The
A B C
of
DOOR to DOOR
VISITATION

By the same author:
THE ABC OF PERSONAL EVANGELISM
THE ABC OF FOLLOW UP
EVERYDAY EVANGELISM
LIFE CHANGE STUDIES 1 & 2

The
A B C
of
DOOR to DOOR
VISITATION

Ron Smith

STL BOOKS
P.O. Box 48, Bromley, Kent, England

STL Books are published by Send The Light Trust,
9 London Road, Bromley, Kent, England.

ISBN 0 903843 07 2

Printed by William Collins & Sons Ltd., Glasgow

Contents

A free copy of this manual will be sent to any full-time Christian evangelist or pastor serving Christ outside the UK, North America or Australasia. Application should be made direct to the author: Ron Smith, Fishers Fellowship, 96 Plaistow Lane, Bromley, Kent, England.

Foreword

Door to door visitation is without a doubt one of the most effective methods of designed outreach evangelism. In the opinion of the author every local church should have a team, no matter how small, that is making contacts for Christ by this method and ensuring that each God-given contact is being carefully and prayerfully followed up.

I have tried to combine practical directions with spiritual principles and Bible teaching. This is why Bible studies appear at the end of most of the chapters. I have for many years been using what I call *Harvester Group Bible Studies,* the most significant feature of which is that every person is given a copy of the notes which they are expected to study *privately* during the week before they come together as a group. A good leader will then have little difficulty in getting group members to participate. The studies in this manual are in most cases *Harvester Group Bible Studies* and are intended to be used in this way.

I was engaged in door to door visitation as a London City Missionary for some fifteen years. I have obviously gathered lessons and materials from many sources. During the past ten years I have been teaching door to door visitation and have learned much from my students. I do not believe we now or ever will have a 'package answer'; it is the responsibility of each local church to see a visitation team formed whose members will pray together, confer together, visit and report in such a way that *many other members,* if not most of the local fellowship, are eventually mobilised into some kind of door to door ministry.

I am very grateful to Mr. Clifford Wadey, one of the elders at East Street Evangelical Church, Bromley, for not only correcting my original manuscript but also offering many valuable suggestions.

My thanks also to my wife Barbara, who has not only been most patient and understanding during the extra hours and attention this book has taken from our lives, but has gone the extra mile and typed out much of the manuscript. Without her, it would not have been written.

Any defect, doctrinal error or unhelpful advice is entirely my responsibility; for any encouragement, scriptural truth or help given in this glorious ministry of door to door visitation, all praise should be given to my Lord. 'To God be the glory'.

Ron Smith.

CHAPTER 1

Principles of
Door to Door Visitation

Often faced with a dwindling congregation of mostly so-far-and-no-farther Christians, and sometimes with a youth group dominated by some anti-establishment, revolutionary inclined leaders, life can be very difficult for a minister today!

In a small congregation the pastor may well decide to give most of his attention to the children's work. This in time should lead to a youth group which, if carefully cultivated, may provide the church of the future. However, in reality, only a small percentage of those who attend the Sunday School will eventually be in any vital church membership. Those who do are mainly those whose parents are church members.

It is an excellent plan to have a systematic visitation programme. Some of us have seen films or read books which tell of mushrooming memberships and the need for extending the premises, but it's amazing how little time the minister can find to actually visit outside of his congregation. His membership may find far less time, even assuming that a small number have the desire and interest to do so. There is also the almost total lack of clear and practical teaching on this fundamental and obvious method of contacting outsiders. Frequently, door to door visitation is designed to invite people who do not have the slightest intention of attending church to pay us a visit! No wonder the few churches who have tried it have found it a difficult and frustrating task.

Then there are those who hold that if only the Word of God is preached faithfully, Sunday by Sunday, the people will come to hear. This might happen if the preacher happens to be a Charles Spurgeon or a Dr. Martyn Lloyd Jones, but even then, those who come usually travel a distance to hear such preaching and are already Christians anyway.

No! The fact is that the outsider cannot be converted by the preaching if he is not there to hear it. Empty pews will not rise up in repentance, and the same dozen or so in the congregation cannot keep on repenting and being saved!

Some believe the answer is prayer. Yes, prayer and yet more prayer. 'Let us have far less of this barrenness of a busy life', they say. 'Let us give ourselves to prayer, more prayer and fasting!' Days of prayer and nights of prayer have been convened, special early morning prayer meetings have been attended by the faithful few, but the situation in the church is unchanged. Obviously the answer includes prayer, but while we pray for a heaven-sent revival, are we to remain otherwise inactive? (No)

Every so often a church council or the deacons will feel the time is ripe for an evangelistic crusade. A well known and respected evangelist will be booked up and the various committees formed. Long hours will be spent in deciding whether the evangelist's face should appear on the posters or not, or exactly how the money is to be raised. Some will join the choir; others will attend the counselling classes; many will give out of a glad and willing heart. Money will be spent on hiring a hall to which the vast majority of the people outside the church will never come. More money will be spent in advertising the crusade meetings, in which most people are not interested. There may well be those who come or just wander in and are wonderfully saved, but most of those who respond will already be within the local church fellowships. Often these are children and young people already under instruction. Outside converts, however, find it difficult to reconcile the bright and informal meetings of the crusade with the few faithful, often elderly, ladies in the church to which they have been assigned! The church members will do their best to welcome them, we hope, but first impressions are very real and can be most offputting to the unchurched. Sometimes the very appearance of our church or hall is against us! Too often our concern for the lost makes us blind as to the cobwebs or peeling paint in the vestry! Overgrown gardens and broken lavatory cisterns do not make the church inviting—in fact many churches have no lavatories! The hardness of the pew, the strangeness of the service, the melancholia of the organ music can all too easily raise mental blocks of resistance, especially in the minds of young people. 'Why don't they worship the Lord with a guitar?' they can be asking themselves.

Years ago many churches had a vital ministry in working class areas by providing some kind of social service— the soup kitchens, the outpatients, mini-hospitals, a bed for the night or shoes for the children running around without any. Times have changed, people are better off, in fact mostly better off than the minister himself. They are no longer interested in secondhand clothing or old toys for their children for Christmas! Although one can still get a queue for a good jumble sale in some areas, or sales of work as they may be called in others, this is no longer regarded as a means of contact for evangelism, but rather a means of raising a few pounds towards church expenses.

Then we have the immigrants in our city centres. Though at first sight they appear to be a good 'field of evangelism', they tend to form their own churches. They import their own peculiar denominational leanings and are rarely inclined to integrate with the existing British churches. We may well be all one in Christ, but we certainly are not all one in church fellowships! We might understand the problems of integration, but we have not found the right answers yet!

Another frustration of the minister is to hear every so often that the brighter and more spiritually alert members are getting more and more involved with a splinter group working outside the church fellowship—a new group, a self-appointed leader, a fresh field of ministry (work among the drug addicts is very popular), a novel doctrinal emphasis or personal experience in which the other members have shared. The cream of our fellowship and of potential workers is suddenly involved in this other interest. What do we do? Talk about the need for loyalty to one's local church fellowship—or join them?

Perhaps we need to come to grips with the situation as

11

it really is. Over the years we have been losing far more than we have gained. We may be evangelical, but we have not been evangelistic! We attend conferences and seminars on evangelism; we read an ever increasing number of books about the subject! If we are honest, we shall admit that we have known the answer all along. It lies quite simply in the mobilisation of our memberships. This involves motivation (desire) and training (direction). Here is the big problem—'How?' How do we motivate our church members into active evangelism? It is at this point that many ministers confuse method with strategy. There are many sure fire methods coming from the U.S.A. at the moment—'How to have a Soul Winning Church', 'Evangelism Explosion', 'Reaching the Man Across the Street', 'Operation Manhunt', 'Every Member Evangelism', 'Christians in Action', etc. They come with handbooks, film strips, study guides, tape recordings, records, questionnaires, self check assignments, even classes on films—all calculated to transform that dwindling few in our congregation to an expanding, outreaching fellowship. Most of them are excellent and, in certain situations, ideal, but the hard fact is that there is no stereotyped, never-miss method of seeing a church begin to multiply itself, other than the personal involvement and day by day communication of Christ by its members. The answer then is not in this method or that method, but in the overall strategy of evangelism of the local church in the local situation by the local Christians.

Methods of evangelism

1 *Church based evangelism*. Sunday services, women's meetings, guilds, men's fellowships, age-group organisations, magazines—this is really in-reach!

2 *Evangelistic crusade*. High cost, often unites churches. Exhibition stands, film rallies—this can be in-reach or outreach.

3 *Coffee bars/Jesus festivals*. These are intended to meet young people on their own ground. Outdate leaseholds, cellars, basements, commons, fields.

4 *Visitation evangelism*. This can include door to door, hospitals, prisons, elderly people's homes,

children's homes.

5 *Literature evangelism.* This can be undertaken by market stalls, colportage work, Press advertising, street distribution.

6 *Open-air preaching.* Always has been and still is a most effective way of gaining contact with those outside and communicating to some.

7 *Social involvement.* Local problems and needs taken up by the church. Concern for the elderly, for the permissive trend, for pollution of the environment.

8 *School opportunities.* Many head teachers welcome responsible Christians to take assemblies occasionally or to show films.

9 *Factory opportunities.* Responsible Christians can sometimes gain entry to visit factories for the purpose of personal counselling.

The basic principles

There must be some method of gaining contact with those who are unchurched. Most Christians, I think, would agree that the best method is the most natural one. What better contacts than the ordinary ones we make in our day to day Christian lives, in our homes, places of business, work or study, just within that orbit of communication where the Lord has placed us? This, however, is not 'doing the work of an evangelist' in the sense in which Paul and the early Christians did it. They *went* where people *were* in order to *make contact* with them *for Christ*. There are some who hold that to make contact with view to evangelise is wrong. If this is true, then it virtually means the end of any kind of out-reach evangelism—and only in-reach evangelism is right. We preach only to those who will come to hear. This principle, however, was not taught by our Lord nor practised by the early Christians. Our Lord plainly said, 'Go ye ... ', and the early Christians plainly 'went everywhere preaching (or making known) the Word'.

We accept the fact then that the best type of contact is the natural one in our day to day Christian living, but we also have a responsibility to *go* where people *are* in order to *make contact* with those who will hear and then *tell them about Jesus.* Sometimes it is possible to make such contacts in secular clubs or places of amusement or sport. A far more likely place, however, is at the door of those who live within walking distance of our church.

The average person is friendly. If asked the time or directions, he will be helpful and willing to co-operate. Similarly when a simple census-card approach was used by visitors from the churches at Chippenham, Wiltshire, 819 willingly answered, giving their church affiliation, and only 289 stated they were not interested. Understandably the average person will be less inclined to listen to talk about something or some One he needs, but he is still less inclined to attend a church to which a stranger is inviting him. This is really expecting too much. The Christian has a large enough problem as it is in communicating the gospel to those who will listen, without adding to it the even larger problem of getting people to a certain place where the communication can be made! The above are fairly obvious considerations, yet how many ministers and Christian leaders think of door to door visitation only as a means of getting the outsider inside! You see this by the way that visitation literature usually consists of letters from 'The Friendly Church', or invitation cards, glossy brochures or leaflets, all portraying some aspect of the church—its modern appearance, its pulpit, the font or even warm hands clasping each other as if to say 'Welcome'. Then follows the usual, 'Our services are. . . .' Such literature might make sense if placed into the hand of a Christian who has moved into the district and is wondering where to go on Sunday. The fact is, however, that no more than 1 in 100 has any intention of attending a church. Approached in this way visitation is bound to be unrewarding, and the tragedy is that some churches have tried this kind of visitation and now judge all door to door visitation to be a waste of time. 'We have tried it', they say, 'and it doesn't work'.

The truth is that door to door visitation is one of the most effective means of gaining contacts for Christ. More contacts can be made for Christ than we can possibly follow through. Problems there are in door to door visitation, but the biggest is how we can find the

14

time to follow through the many God-given contacts we make.

Many books have been written on the subject of door to door visitation, but few give detailed descriptons of methods based upon clearly defined principles. Those that do give detailed descriptions usually take up one method alone. The impression is given that door to door visitation will always be successful if conducted in this or that way. This can be misleading and savours of the 'salesman' approach (the proverbial salesman, that is, not the efficient one). In actual fact there are many different methods of visiting from door to door and many objectives in making the visits. Not only will different methods be more effective in different parts of the country, but also the same can be said concerning different districts in the same town or city. Once the broad principles of door to door visitation are grasped, and several methods considered in detail, then the church visitation team should discover by trial and error which strategy is best in the particular district in which they are working. Individual visitors will also discover which method and general approach they personally feel most free to use. It is only by this trial and report-back method that these variations in the district and personality preferences are discovered.

Visitation according to strength of witness

Some Christians find obtaining the initial contact easier than the communication of the gospel to that person. Others find the opposite; they are able to communicate to a person they have come to know, but find the initial contact difficult. Some, especially younger, Christians would be best employed in simply placing pre-visit letters in the letter boxes. Others can make the personal call a few days later. During the course of visitation, the aged and infirm folk will be discovered. Some members of the visitation team will feel called of God to take on a monthly delivery of a piece of literature, and to have a Bible reading and prayer with such people. These are obviously practical matters which can be discovered and dealt with only through regular reporting, prayer and commonsense discussion.

It would seem wrong to thrust a Christian into face to face witnessing when he is unaccustomed to it. On the other hand many Christians who were full of fears and trembling have been encouraged to try out a simple approach; they have found a new and thrilling avenue of evangelism, which they never dreamed possible. In some way the visitation leaders must be alert to these opposing inclinations and find a way to reconcile them.

One of the greatest helps to the building of an effective visitation team is constant prayer, trial and reports. Before a group of Christians venture out 'on the knocker' to make Christ known, they must first of all come together, learn of Him, pray and take in the Word of God together. This is in fact the basic requisite for all successful visitation, no matter what the method employed. As a general rule at least as much time should be spent in prayer and Bible study together as is spent in calling from house to house. The visitation evening therefore would comprise prayer and Bible study, the visitation itself, and reporting back. Time spent in the presence of the Lord is never out of place, and time spent sharing how the Lord has been with us is always a tremendous encouragement to all present.

The Group Bible Study outlines

The Group Bible Study outlines contained in this book and my other two books in this series *The ABC of Personal Evangelism* and *The ABC of Follow Up* will be found to cover a careful balance of doctrine, devotion and duty. The outlines are intended as group study material, and it is hoped that missionaries, ministers and pastors will reproduce them (translating them if necessary) for use in their local situations.

In a very loose way, the subjects for study are related to the contents of the chapters in the books.

Most of the studies are available in separate sheet form from The Fishers Fellowship, Bromley, Kent, BR1 3AS. A complete list is available upon request.

A copy of the study, either in book form or as a separate sheet, should be made available to each member of the group for private study about a week before the group meeting. This gives opportunity for each person to consider the subject or topic, to look up carefully each reference and other verses and to make such notes as they think helpful. It will be found then that the group meeting becomes alive and informative as each member has previously given thought to the theme of the study.

Suggested programme for the group meeting

✳ 1 Introduction, especially welcoming new members to the group.

✳ 2 Opening prayers, one or two being asked to pray.

✳ 3 The reading around of an appropriate passage or Psalm.

✳ 4 The leader's introductory remarks concerning the subject or topic that is to be studied.

✳ 5 Taking only one section, or even one question at a time, the leader should ask each person in turn for his or her comments upon that section or question.

6 The study material should not be followed rigidly, but fresh and original thought, relative to the theme, should be encouraged.

✳ 7 Endeavour always to finish on time and encourage some to pray at the conclusion of the study.

8 Arrange the time and the place for the next study meeting and ensure each person has a copy of the study paper or of the *ABC* book in which the study occurs.

✳ 9 Light refreshments may be appreciated at this stage, but it is wise not to let refreshments become elaborate, especially if the meetings are being held in different homes each week!

There are 104 studies in all. It is suggested that local leaders obtain a complete list and select subjects in the order in which they would best suit their local requirements. It is not necessary to work through complete sets of the papers.

 Group Bible Study No. 1: Why Win Others? ✳?

Have you prayed first?

In many of our creeds the following statement, or a similar one will be found:

✳'We believe in the resurrection of the body; the final

17

judgment of the world by our Lord Jesus Christ; the eternal blessedness of the believer in Christ and the eternal punishment of the unbeliever. . . .'

Questions:

(a) Do I really believe each of these four statements?

(b) Would they convey vital aspects of the teaching of my church?

(c) About which do I disagree, if any and why?

(d) Am I really concerned about others?

Christianity: The expression of an inner life

(a) That which is hidden; the personal relationship with Jesus Christ . . . *knowing Him*.

(b) That which is seen and heard: the outward expression of that personal relationship . . . *making Him known*.

Christianity: The impartation of a divine mission

Isaiah chapter 6.

(a) Verses 1 to 5. We see God in a new way and are conscious of our own . . . *utter unworthiness*.

(b) Verses 6 and 7. We recognise the provision of God doing for us that which we could not do for ourselves . . . *accepted in Christ alone*.

(c) Verse 8. We understand a mission—we hear the call of God . . . *go into all the world and proclaim*.

Compare the above principles of the impartation of a divine mission with the experience of the apostle Paul (Acts 22: 6-15). Notice how the personal encounter with Christ is followed by a personal witness to Christ. Motivation to evangelism, whether daily witness or door to door visitation, is not something from without *worked up*. It is essentially a new inner relationship *worked out*. Consider this well.

Other sanctions that arise from Scripture

A sanction is a consideration encouraging positive action.

(a) *Indebtedness* (Rom. 1:14) Having discovered or heard good news, we have a moral responsibility to share it. See 2 Kings 7:3-9.

(b) *Command* (Mark 16:15) If we really love the Lord, we shall keep His commandments. He said, 'You shall be my witnesses . . .' (Acts 1:8). And they 'Went every-

where proclaiming . . .' (Acts 8:4).
How is my Church communicating Christ to those out-side today?

(c) *Appointment* (John 15:16) What a privilege to be chosen! But to what purpose? For what reason? What does the word 'fruit' mean here? (See Gen. 1:28, Prov. 11:30 and Rom. 1:13). Is our church being as fruitful for God as it should be? If not why not?

(d) *Compassion* (Rom. 9:1-3) If the love of God, shed abroad in our hearts by the Holy Spirit, does not enable us to feel a longing to reach the lost with the gospel, then something is wrong. What?
How can we, as a company of God's people, regain a divine compassion for the lost that makes us willing to go out, door to door if necessary, to reach them with the gospel of Christ?

Group Bible Study No. 2: Understanding their condition

Have you prayed first?
Read carefully the introductory passage, which is Romans 3:10-23.

The Unconcerned
The average person with whom we live and work day by day is not concerned as to his personal relationship with God. Some may have a form of godliness and even attend church occasionally, but most will be neglectful, un-interested, spiritually ignorant or even antagonistic. Why is Mr. Average-man so unconcerned as to his true condition? Write out your answer before looking up and considering 2 Cor. 4:3,4.

The condition of man without faith in Christ
Discover three implied conditions of natural (or unre-generate) man.
ᶦ (a) Compare Matt. 13:13 with 1 Cor. 2:14.
ᶻ(b) Compare John 8:34 with Romans 7:19.
Ͻ(c) Compare Luke 15:32 with Eph. 2:1.
What other Biblical conditions can you think of?

The work of the Devil
Ever since the fall, the devil has been active to limit the

19

understanding and the ability of man to will, or to do, that which is pleasing to God. List three ways in which this purpose of the devil is being maintained today.

(a) John 17:14-16 and compare Luke 8:14 with 1 John 2:15.

(b) Luke 9:23 and compare Luke 8:13 with 1 Peter 2:11.

(c) Matt. 4:1 and compare Luke 8:12 with 1 Peter 5:8.

Mr. Average-man will therefore esteem his mental and physical desires—for knowledge, the arts, food, drink, recreation, amusement, accommodation and security—the satisfaction or attainment of his mental and physical desires, of far greater importance than meeting the needs of his soul.

How do some Christians try to overcome this natural disinterest a man may have in spiritual matters? To what extent should we trust in such measures? What, if any, are the dangers of using such measures? What, if any, are the dangers of using such means of captivating interest in the things of the Lord?

Conviction of sin—or need of Christ
The first requirement of a man is to experience a realisation of his spiritual need. This sense of need, concern or desire to become right with God is called 'the conviction of the Holy Spirit' (see John 16:8-11). The Holy Spirit is the divine agent of the Godhead who performs his work through the Word of God. Because the Holy Spirit uses the truth of God's Word, Christian workers should know the truth and be able to convey it to others. Discover three ways in which this conviction of God may arise.

(a) Compare Luke 5:8 with Acts 16:30.

(b) Compare Luke 15:18 with Romans 7:18.

(c) Compare Luke 23:42 with Acts 24:25.

Our Lord Jesus Christ said: 'When He is come, He will reprove the world of sin, and of righteousness, and of judgement . . . (John 16:8).

What can we do in order that He may more effectively perform His ministry through us?

CHAPTER 2

Methods of Motivation

Most thoughtful Christians would surely agree that some form of training is required for a local church to reach its maximum efficiency in evangelism outreach. This is why ministers and church leaders arrange teach-ins, days of training, schools of evangelism, weekend house-parties or conferences. Many denominations and not a few societies are constantly convening training ventures in this or that aspect of evangelism. Undoubtedly there are more courses, books, folders, reports and summaries of conferences on evangelism today than there ever has been before! It is relatively easy to obtain knowledge in the various aspects of evangelism, but training alone is obviously not enough. We need to learn how to motivate Christians so that they are not only willing, but wanting to become personally involved in outreach. To give them the 'know how', when they do not have to 'go how', is obviously only part of the needed training. Here, however, we come to a major problem, for only the Lord God can implant in the heart of Christians the earnest desire to make Christ known to others.

Looking at motivation

Why is it that the average Christian is so inactive when it comes to personal outreach? Why is it that of the less than ten per cent of the population who are committed Christians, less than ten per cent of these are making any definite and determined effort to bring Christ to others? The apostle Paul gave himself, stretched, toiled, laboured, travelled, suffered, preached, reasoned, taught and finally died in the cause of knowing Christ and making Him known. He was not alone in such dedication. Throughout the history of the Christian church we can find those who have had such a concern for others that they have done something about it!

Where we have a healthy spiritual life, there will usually be a reaching out, a desire to communicate, a sharing of the heart of Christ concerning those who are lost. The fact and the consequences of sin will be crystal clear. The state and the danger of the sinner will be real and be a burden. The potential and usefulness of a soul will be so vivid that personal outreach will not be a ministry to be encouraged, but rather the natural expression of the daily life in Christ.

It seems we are driven to the conclusion that lack of motivation to evangelise, whether in taking every day opportunities which arise or in making opportunities, such as door to door visitation, is basically a spiritual problem. As with most spiritual problems, the answer will be found only in the ministry of the word and in prayer. The Bible Study outlines, particularly the first two, may be helpful for your group to study in this respect.

Practical reasons for hesitancy in door to door visitation

1 Lack of know how
It is amazing how many Christians let their imagination influence them with regard to door to door evangelism. They imagine that behind every door they will find people who are opposed to them personally and to the Lord Jesus Christ. Others, encouraged by one of the several successful visitation stories, imagine that their church will be full the Sunday after they have visited! Obviously these are extremes, but in between these two, we get all kinds of misconceptions regarding what visitation is really about and what exactly does happen when we go from door to door.

I have found no better exposition of the basic responses than that observed many years ago by that prince of expositors Matthew Henry. He is commenting upon a message in Luke 10. Speaking of the disciples as they went from door to door, he writes:

'Their success would be dependent upon the disposition of those to whom they went. According to whether they were "sons of peace"—so their peace would or would not rest upon the house. The quality of the receiver determines the nature of the reception'.

'*At some houses you will meet "sons of peace"*. Through the previous operations of divine grace they will be ready to receive the Word. Their hearts will have been made as soft as wax, to receive the impressions of the gospel. Such people will be qualified to receive and enjoy the comforts of the gospel. To such homes and people, your peace will rest upon them, your prayers will be appreciated, they will believe the promises of the gospel and begin to enjoy the benefits. The blessings of the gospel will both rest and remain with them—even when you have gone. Your peace shall rest upon that house.

'*At other houses you will meet those who are not so disposed.* You will visit whole houses that have not even one "son of peace" in them. It is very certain that your peace will not come upon them. They have no part or lot in the matter. The blessings that rest upon the sons of peace will never be enjoyed by the sons of Belial. Those who refuse to come under the bonds of the covenant will never enjoy the blessings of it. Your peace in such situations will simply return to you again. But . . . you will have the comfort of having done your duty to God. You have discharged your trust, you have obeyed the Lord. Your prayers like David's will return in blessing upon your own head. Your peace will not rest in that home, but return to you to be communicated to the next home in which you find a son of peace!'

Matthew Henry obviously had the right attitude toward door to door visitation. He did not think so much of the method as the quality of the receiver of the message. So should we. If we adopt this Scriptural attitude then we shall neither be dismayed at the lack of response nor be unduly elated when we are well received.

2 Lack of time

Here is another very practical reason why many Christians do not engage in door to door visitation. They recognise the value of it, they may appreciate the spiritual principles involved, but they just do not have the time to engage in it in the midst of their already overcrowded and busy lives.

The question here is a matter of priority. Every Christian must decide on those things to which they should give priority in their lives. All too often our priorities are determined by our enjoyment rather than our employment. Too many churches spend more time entertaining Christians than engaging Christians.

Jehovah Witnesses, in spite of the hostility they provoke, have built up, and are still building up, one of the most rapidly growing movements simply by means of door to door visitation. They claimed in one year recently to have added 120,000 'home teachers' to the million and a quarter they already had. This alone should make us realise the priority that door to door visitation should have in every Christian church in the land.

It is true that we are busy about many things, but if we are too busy to engage in door to door visitation as a local church, we are neglecting the most effective means of reaching the unchurched for Christ.

3 Lack of leadership

I was reading the other day of an incident where a Christian worker had been trying to witness to a fellow traveller on the plane. The conversation was hard going and the man not particularly interested. The Christian worker then noticed a familiar face and recognised one of America's outstanding Bible conference speakers. He had been invited several times to the Orient to conduct Bible conferences for missionaries. 'I find it means a great deal to them', he told the Christian worker, 'having someone to come from home to the field and share spiritual blessing. It's a new experience for me. As you know, I speak a good deal in conferences back home but have never done anything like this before and I'm finding it one of the highlight experiences of my ministry'. The Christian worker then asked him for some advice in dealing with the disinterested non-Christian. 'How would you go about relating to someone like that?' he asked, hoping for helpful guidance from this seasoned veteran. 'Well', he stammered, 'to be quite candid with you, this is probably one of the weakest areas of my life. I find it easy to get up and speak to a very large audience, but I'm afraid I don't have much success when it comes to the personal encounter!'

There is a remarkable lack of training given in door to door visitation in our theological and Bible colleges. The result is that few ministers have a proper conception of the value of door to door work and still less engage in it. Many visit, of course, but their visitation is too often confined to those who are already members of the church or who are arranging for weddings, baptisms or funerals. Very few ministers will be found persistently and consistently visiting from house to house in order to gain contact for Christ. In many cases they do not have the time for this kind of visiting, because of the many previous contacts they are following up. Therefore not having the experience or the time for consecutive visitation themselves, they can scarcely give a clear lead to their people.

One hesitates to write this, but it is unfortunately true. In conducting visitation training ventures around the country, I find very often the last person I can encourage to go from door to door visiting complete strangers is the minister himself! Almost invariably he has a wedding couple to visit or there is someone else with whom he wants to spend the visitation time.

Helpful facts and statistics to encourage us

'A church with 50 members could cover an area of 5,000 homes (approximately 15,000 people) in three months.' ('Door Bell Evangelism', W.T. Richards). Even as small a number as 40 Christians can reach as many as 1,600 homes in a four-week campaign. Every home will have received a letter and a Scripture portion. Over 300 personal conversations will have taken place and some 320 gospel booklets given to those who have shown a measure of interest. Dozens of contacts will have been made for future visits and some will have even requested that the worker should call again. There are few other ways of making such an impression with the gospel in a district.

In going from door to door we meet with every kind of person imaginable, and we have more opportunities to make a friend and to communicate the gospel than we can possibly obtain in any other way.

When conducting a Christian survey, for example, well over 50% of the people contacted will be willing to co-operate in this. You are far more likely to be invited into a home than you are to meet offence. When using 'Challenge' newspaper, well over 50% of the people will confess to having looked at it, or read it. If you then go on to ask if they would like to receive it every month, 25-30% will confirm that they would, and would be willing to pay for it. During one fairly large-scale visitation venture only 42 were found to be offended out of the 691 persons contacted. Out of the same number 119 invited the worker in!

The response received from visitation when conducted in a prayerful and common-sense way is both surprising and exhilarating. Again and again we have heard Christians confess their utter amazement at the opportunities they have found and the new friends they have made.

A local church working systematically in this way can build up contact with many people in a remarkably short space of time. The problem then becomes one of finding the time to follow through the 'God given' contacts that have been made.

Using the Christian survey approach to visiting, the following very illuminating figures were disclosed:

	Tewkesbury	Croydon	Bromley	Chalk
Number of visitors	28	7	8	13
Number of contacts	203	37	51	88
Invited in	44	19	11	25
Offended at visit	14	2	3	2
Could call again	81	13	19	21
Gospel communicated	72	17	20	20

In a recent Christian survey in Bromley the following answers were received to the six questions asked.

Are you impressed with the works of creation?
① Yes	48
② No	5
③ Don't know	10
④ What do you mean?	6

26

1. Do you believe that there is a Creator God?
   1. Yes — 47
   2. No — 11
   3. Don't know — 8
   4. Sometimes — 1

2. Do you believe it is possible to know God personally?
   1. Yes — 34
   2. No — 27
   3. Don't know — 7

3. Do you believe Jesus Christ died for us?
   1. Yes — 44
   2. No — 12
   3. Don't know — 13

4. Have you experienced the new life that Christ gives?
   1. Yes — 15
   2. No — 35
   3. Don't know — 11
   4. What do you mean? — 1

5. What is a Christian?
   — A person who goes to church — 4
   — A person who believes in God/Christ — 15
   — A person who believes in himself — 2
   — A person who does good to others — 9
   — Don't know — 3

Christian surveys of this nature should always be reported and the responses carefully recorded for all to see. This is a very important aspect of door to door visitation. The Christian survey approach is intended not only as a means of gaining contact and starting a conversation. Such use of a survey is questionable. The great value of a survey is to discover what people are thinking and learn how best to communicate the next time visitation is being undertaken.

How to prepare local Christians for visitation

1   Feed in accurate information concerning visitation
Encourage a small group, which need be only two or three, to research a report for the church on the practical advantages of door to door visitation. Such advantages

27

could be obtained by the members of the group reading books like 'From Door to Door' by D. A. Thrower (Henry E. Walter Ltd.); 'To Every Man's Door' by Maurice Wood (Falcon Booklets); 'Door Bell Evangelism' by W. T. Richards (Christian Witness); and 'Evangelism Explosion' by James Kennedy (Tyndale House).

The work of this group would be to compile a survey on door to door visitation, which would be duplicated and distributed to every member of the church. This could be done over a period of time, each week (Sunday) a report would become available during the given month.

This would serve not only to prepare a nucleus from which a visitation team could be formed at a later date, but also to impart a vision of the importance of this work to the foundation members of the visitation team.

2 Set in motion methods of practical training

The Fishers' Fellowship have for many years been engaged in the task of encouraging and instructing Christians in the task of personal evangelism. Several means of doing this are now available, one or more of which may be adapted for the use of your membership.

(a) The Fishers' Fellowship now provides two sets of a course on personal evangelism, entitled *Winning Another*, in a pack entitled HATWA: 'Help Another Through Winning Another'. Instructions are also provided for the two Christians to meet and work through the course together. This is probably one of the most effective methods of training in personal evangelism. (Details from the Fishers' Fellowship).

(b) Send The Light Trust have 22 cassettes of the Fishers' Fellowship radio programmes, *In Thy Name We Go* . . . . Each of these cassettes contains seven talks on personal evangelism. A complete list of the cassettes is available from Send The Light Trust, 9 London Road, Bromley, Kent.

(c) The group study notes as contained in this manual and in the previous ones, *The ABC of Personal Evangelism* and *The ABC of Follow Up*. There is in fact a great deal of group study material to be found in the three manuals which will provide basic teaching and training in personal outreach. These group study notes are also available as separate sheets from the Fishers' Fellowship office.

(d) Many ministers prefer to run their own 'School of Personal Evangelism' in preparation for a door to door visitation campaign. Some are finding my book, *The ABC of Personal Evangelism* helpful for this purpose.

Any series of training classes or group studies should be carefully planned and the fullest use made of visual aids, home work, scripture memorisation and literature.

3   The principles of effective motivation

We now come to the final stage in motivation which must of necessity involve the Christians in action. Teaching and instruction alone are not enough. They constitute steps in the right direction, but they are only the first steps to start the journey. They must be followed by assignment, action and reports!

Many conferences and teach-ins fail simply because the first two steps only are taken. Christians are taught and instructed, the conference comes to a close, the Christians go home and carry on as usual until the next conference or teach-in.

To follow the teaching and instruction period, there should be planned a definite campaign period, which could be a series of four to six week night ventures of a single day outreach. If a series of evenings is chosen there will obviously be time for only one outreach period each evening. If a Saturday is chosen it is possible to go out at least three times.

It is vitally important that a definite programme is devised and that everyone involved knows exactly where they are expected to visit and what methods they are expected to employ. It is recommended that different methods should be employed and that open discussion after each venture should be encouraged. Elaborate filing systems and collecting statistical information are unnecessary. Some Christian workers tend to overdo the recording of information. It is far better to spend as much as possible of the time you do have together in prayer and the sharing of actual experiences.

In preparing local Christians for a visitation campaign, first give attention to the selection of a research on visitation group. Then have the information gathered by them distributed to every member of your church.

Set in motion a specific means of training, which may need to be basic, covering the fundamentals of the faith, or may need to be more specific, covering a particular aspect of personal evangelism.

You will then need to convene opportunities for personal action and make provision for the hearing of reports from your workers. A final note—do not divide your membership in this kind of venture, but encourage older ones and younger ones to work together.

Discussion questions

(a) What should be considered as the primary objective in visiting from door to door? What other objectives should we have in mind? Who has experiences to share and with what results?

(b) What are the best methods and the reasons for making the initial call? What are the advantages and disadvantages of each method? Who has experiences to share and with what results?

(c) In mobilising a church-based visitation team, what kind of instruction is required? How can this best be imparted in our church? Who has experiences to share and with what results?

(d) In what ways can we communicate the good news of the gospel to those who are willing to listen? What should we do with regard to a friendly contact we have made but where there seems to be no interest in spiritual matters? Who has experiences to share and with what results?

Group Bible Study No. 3: Answering Common Difficulties and Excuses

Have you prayed first?

Those who engage in personal evangelism often encounter problems, difficulties and excuses. At every stage of our ministry—making contact, communicating the good news and presenting a challenge—we shall meet problems which seem to justify doubt or delay.

Both doubt and delay are contrary to the will of God. God commands all men *to repent, to believe* on Christ and to do it *now!* These facts indicate the source of diversions. They may be intellectual and utterly sincere, but they emanate from the enemy of souls!

There is only one safe, sure way of meeting these objections; this is to answer each problem, difficulty or excuse with a *truth* from the *Word of God*.

Answer in writing the following in your own words but using the text truth as a guide

1 'But there is too much to give up'. The Possessive. Mark 8:36.

2 'But how do we know there is a God?' The Atheist. Psalm 19:1.

3 'But I am living a fairly good life'. The Self-satisfied. John 3:3.

4 'But I have gone too far to be saved!' Too far gone. Hebrews 7:25.

5 'But I could never keep it up'. The Hesitant. Phil. 1:6.

6 'But God is too good to damn anyone to hell!' The Optimist. Mark 16:16.

7 'Not now, but I will become a Christian later!' The Procrastinator. 2 Cor. 6:2.

8 'How was the Bible inspired?' The Enquirer. 2 Peter 1:21.

Notice the acrostic P-A-S-T H-O-P-E in the above to aid your memory. There are other intellectual problems which are more correctly called philosophical problems and will be dealt with later. However, these eight are the most common we encounter in our witness for Christ. Write out three others which you think could profitably be discussed at the group study meeting.

Group Study No. 4: Was Jesus Christ Really God?

Have you prayed first?

Many people to whom we speak about Christ will say: 'I agree that Jesus Christ was a good man, but I do not believe that He was God', or, 'Don't you think that Christians have elevated Christ to a false position? He was not really and truly God!' Such remarks as these question a fundamental belief of our Christian faith. If Christ were not God as He claimed to be (John 10:30), then He could never have effected the salvation of others by His death upon the cross. Only God Himself could bear the sins of His creatures; only the just One could suffer in place of us, the unjust! (1 Peter 3:18).

The testimony of Jesus Christ Himself

(a) Notice what He said. He declared Himself to be the Son of God. He claimed equality with God and that His thoughts and actions were the same as those of His Father. He demanded the same honour as the Father (John 5:17-23). He said: 'I and my Father are one' (John 10:30). At His trial He asserted that He was the Christ, the Son of God (Matt. 26:63-66). He affirmed His pre-existence (John 17:5) and that whosoever had seen Him had seen the Father (John 14:9). What else did He say about His deity?

(b) Notice what He did. There is divine authority in His sayings that is found in those of no other man. Christ instantly answered the most difficult questions in such a way that they are settled for all time. Christ healed with a word or a touch and the cure was complete. When a storm arises it will run its course, but when Jesus spoke, immediately there was great calm. He fed the multitude with five loaves and two small fishes. He raised the dead by a call or a touch. What else did Christ do that can only be accounted for by His deity?

The testimony of His influence through the ages

(a) Notice His influence upon music and art. Consider any person who has ever lived throughout the whole of human history. Who else has inspired so many paintings, hymns, poems and melodies? More books have been written about Jesus Christ than about any other person in the world past or present.

(b) Notice His influence upon His disciples. After the death and resurrection we see men transformed! The death of Christ left them despondent and disillusioned—Luke 24:21. In the Acts, however, they emerge as men who hazard their lives for the name of the Lord Jesus Christ and who turn the world upside down!

(c) Notice His influence upon men and women

throughout history. Vast multitudes have testified and will do so today if asked: 'Christ made the difference. My life was full of sin and wretchedness; I had no point or purpose in my life; I tried many man-made systems of religion and philosophy; I then came under the influence of Jesus Christ. I had a personal encounter with Him. He is now transforming my life!'

The testimony of personal experience
Human reason can indicate just some of the testimonies by which we can concede that Jesus Christ is certainly different from any other man. It is possible even to accept intellectually that He is the Son of God. Yet no amount of reasoning can make Christ *real* to a person. He still says: 'Come unto Me . . . Learn of Me . . . Follow Me . . .' and those who respond by faith to His invitation will find Him true to His Word. They will discover, as Peter or Paul did, an inner conviction resulting from divine revelation: 'Thou art the Christ, the Son of the living God', affirmed Peter, and: 'Lord, what wilt Thou have me to do?' asked Paul.

The early Christians never questioned the deity of Jesus Christ; although quite early in the history of the church this became a target for heretical teachings about which both Paul and John had to give warning (1 Tim. 1:3 and 10, and 1 John 2:22, 4:13-15).

Write a brief statement (about 200 words) suitable to be read out at your next group meeting, 'Why I believe Jesus Christ is God'. Also compose two questions which seem to imply that He could not be God, together with helpful replies.

Group Bible Study No. 5: Why did God allow sin to enter creation?

Have you prayed first?
'But if sin is the cause of all the trouble in the world, why did God allow sin to come into the world anyway? God must have known the havoc that it would cause!' Such remarks question either the wisdom of God or the power of God to control the universe which He has created (Genesis 1:1). God created all things. Does this

mean God created sin? See Isaiah 45:7 and compare several versions.

We should begin by understanding that the Bible does not cause sin. The Word of God, however, claims to reveal it (Romans 7:7). Sin would exist and does exist whether the Bible is accepted, rejected or unknown (Romans 1:18,19; 2:14,15). Sin is the transgression of the law, and the ability to transgress the law is part of man's constitution. Whoever created the world and made man—permitted sin to come in and mar it. We should also understand exactly what sin is; put the following definitions of sin in your own words: 1 John 3:4; James 4:17; John 16:9.

Is man a robot or a creature with the capacity to choose?
The answer is obviously the latter and the Bible is emphatic about the implications. God has made man as a free, moral agent and always deals with man as a being with a will of his own. Man is normally able to choose either God's way or his own way. Here are the alternatives and God's plea, 'I have set before you life and death, blessing and cursing: Therefore choose life' (Deut. 30:19).

Is it possible to love God without the freedom to choose? Is it possible always to choose the right when we are able to choose the wrong? Why don't we always choose the right?

The Scriptures indicate the origin of sin and evil
Sin originated in Satan's fall, through pride and rebellion. See Isaiah 14:12-15 and compare Proverbs 16:18. Sin entered the world through Adam and Eve. See Romans 5:12,19 and Genesis 3:6. 'To remove the possibility of sin it would be necessary either to destroy man's free will or to repeal all law'. Discuss this. If there were no laws would evil cease to exist? If no one had the ability to choose except God would sin be possible?

We need not speculate unduly concerning the origin of sin
If your mother were critically ill, would you call for a doctor or speculate first how she caught the infection or how the disease germs came to be in the world in the first place?

The non-Christian has no real answer to the fact of sin
Unbelief does not destroy the fact of moral evil or prevent the practice of it. Indeed, unbelief often encourages it! The unbeliever abolishes sin (to his own satisfaction) only by reducing man to an animal, ignoring it, permitting it or call it by other names. The fact of sin and the results of sin are still to be seen. The non-Christian has no supreme King, no law by which to reveal sin or to warn of its consequences. He therefore has no motive to holiness other than the social conscience. If a non-Christian is found to live a morally upright life, and of course many do, this will more often than not be found to be due to his upbringing and early training. These will generally be found to be based upon Christian principles of an earlier generation (Proverbs 29:15). Discuss this. What motives will cause a non-Christian to live a godly life?

The character of God is abundantly vindicated
by His provision
If mankind were faced solely with the problem of sin, the unbeliever might have a case. But God has also revealed the cure for sin. God gives many promises of blessing to the pure and holy, all of which tend to keep men from sin. God has caused to be written for our learning lessons from the lives of those who have gone before us both bad and good. Yet He has done more. God has provided a remedy for sin, the world's most awful disease, in the person of our Lord Jesus Christ. Forgiveness and pardon are offered to those who believe in Him. To understand the divine power is something granted to those who encounter Him by faith and trust in His indwelling presence. Discuss this. What other provision for sin can we find in this world?

Can we rightly question God as regards the sin which He permits (by making us creatures with free will) in view of the full provision He has made in the gift of His Son, our Lord and Saviour?

CHAPTER 3

Methods of Visitation

The word 'visitation' comes from the same root as the word 'vision'. It means to go and see someone, to extend friendship, comfort or help. Proverbs 29:18 tells us, 'Where there is no vision the people perish'. Is it not equally true 'Where there is no visitation, the people perish?' With regard to Christian visitation, the visitor should have as his primary objective the communication of the good news of the gospel. Merely to make friends is good, but is not good enough. Some visitors stop short at the mere social call. Ministers are often guilty of this; a friendship is established and they know a welcome is always extended. This may be with a parent of a Sunday School scholar or with a young couple who were married in the church, but the visit never becomes an evangelistic opportunity!

There are hundreds of scriptural illustrations which teach us that visitation is the basic means of reaching people. In Genesis 3 we read of God who visited Adam and Eve in order to restore the fellowship that had been broken by sin. In Judges 6 the Lord visits Gideon to announce that he would be used to lead Israel against her enemy. In Daniel 3 it is recorded that a person whose form was like the 'son of God' visited the three Hebrews in the burning fiery furnace. So we could go on. The Lord Jesus Christ visited as a major feature of His earthly ministry. We often forget this. He did not invite people to come and hear Him; He did not (as far as we know) distribute literature; He did not broadcast, although He did speak to crowds and even multitudes upon occasions. Jesus Christ made a point of moving among people, visiting them by the sea shore, in the highways, at the gates of their cities, and in their homes.

The Lord has commanded His people in every age to 'go'. The New Testament epistles clearly teach that visitation was, and should be, the basic means of contacting people. Paul wrote to Timothy 'The things that thou hast heard of me among many witnesses, the same commit thou to faithful men, who shall be able to teach others also' (2 Timothy 2:2). Here the pattern is established. One tells another, who tells another, who tells another and so on.

Romans 10 also emphasises the importance of visitation. Several difficult questions are asked. How can people call upon Christ if they have not heard about Him? How can they hear about Him unless someone is sent from the Lord to them? Paul could say, 'But they have not all obeyed the gospel', referring to the non-Christian. Well might we say today, 'But they have not all obeyed God's command!' referring to the Christian! The Lord desires to send us each one to make contacts for Christ, and what better or more scriptural means can be found than visitation?

Visitation according to individual strength

There are some brave souls who can start a conversation about Christ within a few sentences with a minimum of embarrassment upon either side. They are, however, in the minority! Most Christians, some obviously more than others, recognise a certain amount of individual threat. All kinds of factors can determine this, both known and unknown. This means that the actual 'witness-barrier' is harder to penetrate for some Christians than for others.

Ideally, perhaps a healthy, spiritually adjusted Christian should find no difficulty in communicating Christ. He should therefore need no aids and should regard even the printed page as a secondary means of communication. In visiting he should simply tell the person on the doorstep he would like to talk about the Lord and he should trust the Holy Spirit as to whether the visit leads to fuller communication or not.

We have to recognise though that even a healthy, spiritually adjusted Christian will not in every instance consider that the 'direct approach' is either appropriate or the best. Most Christians, indeed, if taught the 'direct approach' and expected to employ it every time, would experience all kinds of mental resistance—some justified, some not!

It is for these basic reasons, the personality differences of Christians, that we believe there is no short or slick method of visitation which everyone should use and which will be best employed in every place. We shall therefore now give our attention to eight basic methods and consider some of the advantages and disadvantages of each.

Method 1: The direct approach

We have been commanded to go, to share with people where they are, to make contact with them and where possible to communicate the gospel. It is therefore quite understandable that some Christians find it best to go straight to the point when they visit a home. For example, as the door is opened they would say: 'Good evening, I'm Ron Smith, I am a member of such and such a church, and I would like to speak to you about the Lord Jesus Christ . . .'

There are many things to be said for this kind of approach to visitation. There is a simple and artless directness about it; we say what we mean and we mean exactly what we say. No one can accuse us of being devious and of all the methods we shall consider it is probably the most scriptural.

There is obviously a greater individual threat experienced by the visitor and the number of refusals to continue the conversation will probably be greater than if other methods are used.

The Lord will undoubtedly use the ministry of the worker who adopts this direct approach, but we have to recognise two facts: not all Christians will feel at ease using it, and in many cases we must earn the right to be heard and this will take time, possible many visits.

Method 2: The Christian survey

First let us be quite clear that it is a genuine survey we

are conducting. Following such a visitation venture, the results should be collected and set out in visual form for all to see. It helps tremendously to know what the average person is thinking concerning God, Christ, the world, human needs, salvation and how to find acceptance with God.

Obviously in the actual conducting of the Christian survey the worker may be given the opportunity to express his own view, but this should not be forced in any way. The Holy Spirit is well able to change the direction of the conversation from a general discussion to specific, spiritual matters.

The Christian survey questions need careful thought. One of the 'secrets of success' is to have no more than five or six questions in all. It is also helpful to have them printed on a card.

It will be found that about sixty per cent of people are willing to co-operate in answering such a survey. Although the survey approach causes more offence than most of the others (except the direct approach), it will be found that more workers are invited into homes when this method is used than any other method.

Method 3: The use of Challenge or a monthly magazine

The Good News Paper *Challenge* is distributed with an introductory letter, explaining who has sent it and that the visitor will be calling again in a few days to see if it is wanted regularly each month. Some teams deliver three or four copies of *Challenge* before making the call. It is a very interesting form of communication for certain areas. About forty-five per cent will be found to have read it, or parts of it, and some twenty per cent will be willing to have it delivered regularly. Most will be quite willing to pay for it! The advantage is that those who request it give us a reason for calling each month, friendships are encouraged and the setting of communicating the gospel becomes natural.

The Anglican churches have a certain advantage in commending the Parish Magazine. To make a call from 'your church' and to ask if the person would like to become a subscriber to the Parish Magazine will bring an even greater response than is obtained from a *Challenge* distribution. These contacts, however, must be faithfully followed through.

There is still need for a well produced 'glossy monthly' designed to appeal to the non-Christian and providing a high standard of Christian news and views, information and even stories that might be acceptable in certain areas where *Challenge* is not so well received. Even twelve undated issues of such a magazine would be helpful in establishing contact and making new friends over the course of a year.

Method 4: The sale of literature

This is a method again more suited to some Christians than others. We can present outselves as calling on a 'Good Literature Crusade', and express our concern over the increase of degrading books available today. If we really love people, we shall be interested in them. Ask questions to demonstrate that interest. Show courtesy in listening to what they have to say.

It is best to have with you only six or seven titles, e.g. 'Basic Christianity' (John Stott), for those who would profess to be 'Church of England'; 'Peace with God' (Billy Graham)—Many have seen or heard about Billy Graham and the mention of his name often starts a natural conversation about spiritual matters; 'Starting from Zero' (Metcalf Collier) for the very thoughtful type of person. Then several children's books will be useful. Also, you might like to carry a selection of the 'Answer' booklets (Victory Tract Club), giving an answer to worry, loneliness, defeat, fear, death, guilt, depression and other conditions.

If you find a person who seems to have no real interest in a book, remember that the insurance man offers protection and peace of mind, not policies! The travel agent promises romance, adventure, the holiday of a lifetime, not tickets! The toothpaste manufacturer 'sells' freedom from decay, instant whiteness, and try the tongue test! In the Bible are found the answers to man's deepest needs; spiritual books help to make these relevant answers today! Talk therefore of peace, security, love, forgiveness, life, purpose.

After fairly extensive visits, using all the methods described, this has proved to be the least encouraging of all. Even so, twelve or thirteen books are likely to be sold at every one hundred homes visited. Those who buy the books are more likely to read them, and we have found that most people who refuse to purchase a book readily accept a tract or copy of John's Gospel.

Method 5: Invitation to a local home

We have already considered the inadvisability of inviting a person to a church service, but an invitation to a home is more likely to be accepted, especially in a rural area where houses are scattered and people are more likely to know each other. The term 'meeting' should be avoided, and preferably a term such as 'After Eight', 'Pop Inn', or 'Talk Back' should be used. Of all the methods used, this was the most revealing and encouraging. Of those who were visited, twenty-one per cent expressed an interest in such an 'At Home'. Twenty-five complete strangers actually attended one of the discussion evenings out of the 690 homes visited. It would appear that, for every 100 visited, 21 will show interest and 3 or 4 will actually attend a local home discussion. It must be remembered that many of these visits were in rural areas.

Method 6: Visiting to enrol children or young people

This method was among those causing the least offence. People are always happy to talk about their children, but where these had grown up, or where there were no children, the visitors reported a barrier to further conversation. This method, however, is very useful for the training of new workers in door to door visitation and for the building up of the Sunday School or Youth Group.

The purpose of the visit is simply to enquire if there are children (or it may be young people) in the home who might like to know about, and be invited to, our Sunday School (or the new coffee bar we are starting).

It will have been noticed that each method of visiting

adopted will provide a different kind of opportunity for the presentation of the gospel. Generally speaking, the more direct the approach the more likely you are to find yourself speaking to a person about Christ.

Recommendations from the Chilterns Crusade Visitation Work

1 That many Christians, possibly in your church, would visit if given definite and limited objectives.

2 That the more mature counsellor-trained Christians will witness for Christ quite naturally.

3 That prayerful, intelligent visiting on behalf of your church or assembly will generate more good will than offence.

4 That home meetings and discussion groups can reach complete strangers and bring them into fellowship, first in the home, later in the church.

5 That a series of training classes is a most valuable 'lead in' to a visitation venture, especially when discussion groups are encouraged and problems freely shared.

Method 7: Booklet distribution—with call back

Many churches are undertaking a booklet distribution of certain sections of their town or city. A 'Gospel in Every Home' Crusade is one idea. The PTL Gospels are very useful for this purpose. They are printed in the Living Gospel version, have a simple 'bridge' illustration in the final pages and contain a pre-paid card which can be completed and returned to the PTL by anyone who would like to receive further help. This particular method of visitation is usually preceded by a letter and then the Gospel or the booklet is 'presented' during the call a few days later. Results will vary tremendously according to the personality of the worker and the way in which he presents the booklet. If he is a little timid, and feels it right to 'offer' a copy of the Living Gospel, he may well find that the majority of the people say, 'No, thank you!' or 'I'm not interested'. Many workers have returned to say, 'We can't even give them away!' Another type of worker, however, will adopt a different approach and say, 'I've come from such and such Church and there is your copy of the Living Gospel we promised . . . '. Then he will report later that not only were most copies accepted, but also several very interesting conversations resulted!

Other useful booklets with which to 'blanket cover' an area are: 'The Reason Why' (the new edition by Contact for Christ); 'Journey into Life' (Falcon Books); and 'Opening the Door' (Victory Tract Club). It is very satisfying when a visitation team can work together, praying and patiently distributing, and then look back several months later to realise that whole sections of their community have been covered with gospel literature in this way. There will undoubtedly be many opportunities too for personal conversation.

Method 8: Literature distribution—without a call back.

Some church visitation teams have 'blanket covered' whole sections of their town or city with suitable literature. No call back is made at all and so of course the personal contact is rarely made. Among the main advantages of this method is the fact that almost any Christian in the church can be mobilised to the simple task of placing prepared literature into letter boxes and, given only, say, ten workers, several streets can be covered at a time.

This particular method of visitation (although strictly speaking it does not involve actual visiting in the normal way) was adopted by three churches in Dundee. Following a 2-3 week campaign it was estimated that 99.8% of the non-Christians were untouched. It was suggested that if a campaign were run in a neutral hall in conjunction with other Christians they would feel well rewarded if 1,000 non-Christians heard the gospel. This would still leave 99% of Dundee's 100,000 untouched by the gospel!

A new approach was thought out, and ten three minute 'talks' on cards were prepared and the idea was to distribute two of the cards each week over a period of time. Distributing 'Challenge' a worker averages 15 calls per hour, with the visitation cards he can manage 120 in 30 minutes! This means that 16 of his 'Get Right with

God' cards can be distributed in the time it takes to hand over one 'Challenge'.

If a Christian worker is willing to give two hours weekly, (not including travelling time) he could deliver cards to 400 flats. Later in the week someone else, also giving two hours, could deliver the next card in the series to the same 400. If a few churches between them produced only 20 people who would volunteer to give two hours weekly, then 8,000 calls could be made each week. Thus in five weeks the whole 4,000 flats would have been reached with the ten cards. I can leave my reader to work out how many homes could be covered with literature in the same campaign period if 50 people were participating from a number of churches!

There are, of course, many variations in both literature and frequency for such forms of distribution. It will be realised that results may not be seen from this type of work and in many cases the literature will be only a link somewhere in the chain that may eventually lead to a person's conversion. *If no other outreach visitation programme is being pursued from your church, this one should at least be considered!*

The pre-visit letter

We have now considered several actual methods or reasons for making the call. Each will involve a different degree of individual threat to the visitor and different methods will be suited to different areas. Some visitation teams make provision for the visitors to choose which of two or three methods they prefer. Sometimes the best method is a combination of two or even three methods.

Opinion varies with regard to the value of a pre-visit letter. It is true that in many homes the pre-visit letter is not even read and in some cases, depending upon the type of letter and the person who receives it, it may even prevent a useful visit rather than prepare for one!

All things considered, however, such a letter can be a help rather than a hindrance if it is carefully written and attractively duplicated or printed.

(a) It should be pleasing in appearance, yet not flashy and need not be the multicoloured variety which immediately implies we have something to sell. On the other hand, it should not be cheap and shoddy.

(b) The contents should be interesting to the non-churchgoer and be relevant to situations today. Some prefer to make a straight challenge to consider spiritual issues in view of the state of the world today; others will express the Christian viewpoint on some national or local news. The reason for the visit should be clearly stated. Some letters assure the occupant that the visitor is not a member of one of the sects and would welcome an opportunity to speak about spiritual issues if given the opportunity.

There are many kinds of pre-visit letters and a selection of the latest is usually obtainable from the Fishers Fellowship office. The following is a standard one, the final paragraph of which will need to be changed according to the method of visitation that is being used.

Dear

Is it not true that there is a greater unity in home life today, that crime is decreasing and that mankind in general is becoming more peaceful, more reliable, more truthful and better in every way? Unfortunately it is not! Many thoughtful people are becoming concerned about the way of the world. Strikes and violence abound, family life seems to be breaking up, moral standards are being discarded and some of today's youth seem to be in rebellion against organised society.

Politics, education, demonstrations help but little. We believe, however, there is an answer, there is hope. Christians have always believed that the answer to both national and personal problems is to be found in a Person—the Lord Jesus Christ. What a different place this world would be, for example, if everyone were a Christian in the true sense of the word. Have you ever wondered what makes a person a true Christian?

We as a church are concerned about these matters and are organising a Christian survey to find out exactly what people think about these problems and to show how God and His church have something relevant to say and to do in this present situation.

In a day or so I shall be calling to ask your help in completing a simple survey. Your co-operation in this will be very much appreciated. I do hope you will be prepared to spare a few moments of your time. Your answers will be confidential (we shall not even require your name) but when considered with others they will help us to communicate the Christian message which we believe is the only hope for the world today.

Looking forward to meeting you personally,

Church visitor

Some visitation teams may wish to obtain the names of the persons to be visited and type them at the head of the letters. Another help, I think, is to place the letter in envelopes, ready addressed. Other churches we know have even posted the letters!

Preparing for visitation

Obviously some kind of preparation for visitation will need to be made by the leading member of the visitation team. A well thought out and prayerfully executed plan of campaign is more likely to meet with a measure of success than haphazard visiting with no clearly defined objective or control.

The personnel

Thought will need to be given to the preparation of the visitors. Some kind of training would be helpful and the overall strategy should be in the nature of a period of preparation, a period of visitation and then a period of consolidation. Training could be by means of a series of studies in personal evangelism relative to door to door work before the visitation itself. But it will be found that some of the best training is received when actually engaged in the task and then reporting back to each other. The Fishers Fellowship have a series of group study notes, entitled *Time to Advance*. These studies introduce a very simple method of approach using 'Challenge' newspaper; the advantage of these notes is that actual assignments are suggested as the group is working through the studies and the idea of the group sharing experiences is being encouraged week by week.

The area

One of the big mistakes made by many churches contemplating visitation is to think in terms of saturating an area, rather than dissecting it and taking a little at a time! One author teaching door to door evangelism talks in terms of reaching 20,000 homes. He assumes a church has 200 adult members and suggests that the area be divided into six or seven districts, each having a district superintendent in charge of 6 to 12 workers. This of course is assuming that 36 to 72 members of that church are willing to participate in such a visitation programme. One well known suburban church with over 300 in membership could scarcely muster 20 members for even a day's visitation work, and many of those were young people!

It is helpful then to obtain a large-scale ordnance survey map of the area, to select a particular district which may only be three or four streets and then to get a copy of the local electoral roll which covers just those streets. In this way a more realistic section is being envisaged in relation to the number of people you expect to comprise your visitation team. It is best to have a smaller section and cover it.

The time and period of visitation

The allocation of time will need to be considered in the light of your local situation. Will your visitors come together for one day, pray together, study, and visit say for one period in the morning, one in the afternoon and another early evening? Between times will they have meals together and share reports after each venture? Another suggestion is to set aside a visitation campaign period, four, six or ten weeks perhaps. On the same evening each week the visitors meet, pray, study, visit and share reports. It is recommended that the visitation does not continue indefinitely, at least not at this first operation.

The day or the period of visiting is intended to introduce the workers to the ministry and to gain 'God-given' contact, which should be followed up as we shall see later.

The third arrangement is to combine a visitation venture with the existing mid-week meeting. The mid-week meeting is used as the occasion when visitation packs are distributed (each containing material and directions for visiting 10 to 15 homes); the actual visitation is done at any time during the week according to the time available or set aside for the purpose by the individual worker. The reports on the visitation are given at the next week's mid-week meeting. Again this programme should not be allowed to continue too long; rather it should be looked upon as a definite period of outreach by the church.

The materials

Materials will vary according to the methods being used: pre-visit letters, Gospels, booklets, survey-cards, copies of *Challenge* etc. It will be found helpful if the materials can be made up in advance as packs suitable to visit ten or fifteen homes.

The matter of records is one which can easily be over done! We have seen some that are very involved and the information required is rarely used. In fact the obtaining of the information can easily detract from the communication of the gospel. All that is needed is an index card, containing the name and address of the person to be visited. Following the visit the worker should simply add the date when the visit was made, a sentence to indicate response and one star to indicate 'Generally a friendly reception', two stars 'Interested *could* call again', or three stars, 'Very interested, God-given contact, *should* call again.'

The opening remarks

We are going to assume the pre-visit letter has been sent; you understand the purpose of your visit; the team have prayed and read the Word together; and now you are approaching the home for your first visit.

Often we are asked if it is better to visit in pairs or singly. Obviously to visit in pairs requires less courage on the part of the visitors, and it can be a means of training the less experienced. The fact is, however, that two visitors confronting the one person who opens the door does put him at a disadvantage. It is one of those open questions; some Christians find they can work better with a friend, while others find that the person tends to be more friendly and certainly discusses spiritual matters more freely, when he is speaking to only one person.

Male and female partners can be a cause of personal problems—especially if a husband and wife from different families insist on working together. Some team leaders therefore insist upon choosing the partners. A simple rule could be never to work with the same partner of the opposite sex more than once. In the USA I understand they avoid this kind of problem by sending out the visitors three at a time.

First impressions are very important. We should therefore be clean, suitably dressed and present ourselves courteously and cheerfully. Then comes that tense moment when we ring the bell or raise the knocker—a good time to commit that particular visit to the Lord.

It may sound a very obvious thing to mention, but it is so often overlooked by a timid visitor—the cheerful smile goes a long way to encourage a friendly reception. The opening remarks are important too.

'Good evening Mr (Occupant)'.

'I am Mr (Visitor) calling on behalf of (Name of Church) and the Christian Survey which we are conducting. Would you be so kind as to answer a few questions on our card here?' At this point it is helpful to show the card and to flick through some of the cards previously answered. The person then realises that the card contains only a few questions and notices that several people have answered them already.

We are assuming here that the Christian Survey methods is being used, but a similar straightforward approach should be employed with other methods. We do not want to imply that we must trust in psychological, salesman techniques, but common courtesy and sincere compliments are surely in order. 'You have a lovely garden!' 'What a beautiful little girl—how old is she?' If people are rude, then smile and apologise for disturbing them.

You may need to overcome anything that might prejudice them against you such as thinking that you are a Jehovah's Witness or Mormon, that you are going to attack their religion, that you are assuming you are better than they, or that you are some kind of religious fanatic. It will help you to overcome such prejudices by speaking in a quiet, friendly, simple manner—and be very sincere.

Following the initial contact, you move into stating the purpose of your visit. In doing so however, you must be alert to the God-given opportunity of witnessing to Christ. Remember many people for a long time now have been misinformed through the mass media as to exactly what the church is or does. If challenged upon the usefulness or value of the church, it is best to admit its defects where they are valid, but then turn the conversation to Jesus Christ, asking for views about Him.

Sometimes a worthwhile conversation will quite naturally begin, but if it becomes unduly protracted it may be wise to excuse yourself, (as you may have several more visits to make that evening), but ask if you can call again and what time would be convenient. On the other hand never close a promising conversation for visits elsewhere, which may not prove fruitful.

Often a useful starter to a conversation is briefly to explain how you personally became a Christian. If you were converted as a child however, be careful that you do not in effect 'talk down' to people by being over simple. A personal testimony is likely to be more helpful than repeating the apostles' creed or programming the person through one of the popular *Bridge of Life* illustrations. These communication materials have their time and place, but they ought not to be used as a kind of package-deal presentation. We must avoid the slick presentation of the irreducible minimum of the gospel and imagining we have effectively communicated the message as soon as we have cornered a person into hearing an *ABC of Salvation*. This is not personal evangelism—it could be nearer amateur brain washing!

When visiting try to be relevant, practical, realistic and brief. Avoid theological terms as far as you possibly can but use simple illustrations from everyday life to make your points. Speak clearly, in a friendly way and show controlled enthusiasm. Never talk down to a person, never be sarcastic, never use ridicule, and never apologise for the message you proclaim. Look upon every person who answers the door to you as a potential contact arranged by God Himself. You are not expected to 'sell' the Lord; simply speak about Him. You have nothing to collect, but you have everything to give.

One of the basic rules in door to door visitation, besides prayerfulness, is to recognise the value of and to practise the art of listening. It is true we have only one answer to every human need, the deepest being sin, and all have sinned. Nevertheless, we should always try to meet the person at the 'faith point' or 'doubt point' where they really are, rather than where we think they ought to be. This will mean listening, understandingly and it will take time. Therefore visitation is not a 'hurry task'. People should not be regarded as potential souls to be placed in our 'bag'. Someone has said, 'We are called to be fishermen, not scalp hunters!' Therefore every visit is a venture and an experience of standing with Christ and in His Name at the door of a home. Like marriage, it is not to be taken up lightly, but reverently.

The pull away appeal

On concluding a visit, which may take one minute or one hour, we should thank a person for being helpful, if appropriate of course, and commend suitable literature as we leave. It is usually possible to give every person at least a helpful tract; some could also be given a John's Gospel or other helpful booklet. Always endeavour to leave the person a little closer to Christ than he was when you called. You may feel in some situations that you can ask the person if a call back could be made, or even should be made.

The three aspects of making a call should be given careful thought and discussed in your team meetings from time to time. The opening encounter, the purpose of the visit, and the pull away appeal, leaflets, booklets, future visits, whether possible or highly desirable.

Group Bible Study No. 6: Prophecy—Evidence for Bible Inspiration

In both my other books there are Group Bible Studies on

the subject of *Bible inspiration*. Here we are simply listing a number of prophecies concerning our Lord Jesus Christ, all of which came true.

What is a prophet?

A prophet is a spokesman for God. To prophesy means to proclaim or to declare. In one sense a prophet was a 'forthfeller' who declared what God had to say to his contemporaries. In another sense he was a 'foreteller', because his words had a predicative meaning. He told what would happen in the future. Some of the prophecies listed in this study were written 600 to 700 years before their fulfilment! List for discussion at your group meeting (a) five prophets of the Bible together with five of their prophecies (not using any of the prophecies in this study), and (b) the ways in which such revelations were received.

Prophecies about the lineage of Jesus Christ

The seed of the woman.	Gen. 3:15.	Luke 2:7.
The line of Shem.	Gen. 9:26.	Luke 3:36.
The tribe of Judah.	Gen. 49:10.	Luke 3:33.
The seed of Abraham.	Gen. 12:3.	Matt. 1:1.

Prophecies about the birth of Jesus Christ

His deity—Son of God.	Isa. 7:14.	Matt. 1:22,23.
His humanity—Son of Man.	Psa. 8:4-6.	Heb. 2:5-9.
His mother a virgin.	Isa. 7:14.	Matt. 1:18.
His name.	Isa. 7:14.	Matt. 1:21,23.
His birth place.	Micah. 5:2.	Luke 2:4-7.

Prophecies about the ministry of Jesus Christ

His forerunner.	Isa. 40:3.	Matt. 3:1-3.
His anointing.	Isa. 11:2.	John 1: 33, 34.
His office as prophet.	Deut. 18:18,19.	John 12:49.
His office as king.	Zech. 9:9.	Matt. 21:1-9.
His office as priest.	Psa. 110:4.	Heb. 5:5-8.

Prophecies about the death of Jesus Christ

His betrayal.	Psa. 41:9.	John 13:18.
His abandonment.	Zech. 13:7.	Matt. 26:31-56.
His silence.	Isa. 53:7.	John 19:9.

His maltreatment.	Isa. 50:6.	Matt. 26:67.
His persecutors.	Psa. 2:1,2.	Acts 4:24-28.
His crucifixion.	Psa. 22:16.	Matt. 27:35.
His garments.	Psa. 22:18.	John 19: 23,24.
His intercession.	Isa. 53:12.	Luke 23:34.
His cry.	Psa. 22:1.	Matt. 27:46.
The gall and vinegar.	Psa. 69:21.	Matt. 27:34.
The side pierced.	Zech. 12:10.	John 19:34-37.
His bones not broken.	Psa. 34:20.	John 19:33-36.
His burial.	Isa. 53:9.	Matt. 27:57-60.

Some have estimated the chances of the occurrence of each event prophesied. This has given them a probability figure. They have then multiplied each probability figure with the next in turn to discover the overall chances of them all coming true. This has of course resulted in an astronomically large figure. We have, however, listed only twenty-seven of the calculated three hundred and thirty-three prophecies concerning our Lord Jesus Christ! To any fair minded person coincidence cannot explain this. The Christian accepts the fact that divine inspiration alone can account for such detailed prophecies as these.

It must be remembered when speaking to a person who doubts the inspiration of Scripture, we cannot force a man to believe by reason. There are sufficient reasons (prophecy is only one) upon which a man can build a structure of confidence, but the weight of reason cannot compel faith in the man who is saying, 'I will not believe!' The real problem behind unbelief is not arithmetical or philisophical, but moral.

Question for your group discussion:

If you were an unbeliever, how would you explain all these prophecies?

Group Bible Study No. 7: What About Those Who Have Never Heard the Gospel?

Have you prayed first?

We sometimes encounter the problem: 'But what about the person who has never heard of Jesus Christ and salvation, will he be condemned to hell?'

God is just
Of one thing we can be absolutely certain, that God is just and will never act out of character. His ways of fairness and right dealing, however, while perhaps not different from ours are infinitely higher than ours.

A Christian believes that just as the works of God in creation are exact and precise, so the ways of God are morally pure. We do not believe that God will condemn any person unjustly. In point of fact 'all have sinned and come short of the glory of God' (Rom. 3:23). Enoch and other Old Testament characters, however, who have never heard the gospel as we know it, found a place of acceptance with God through faith. Every one, however, is accepted on the basis of the atoning work of Jesus Christ, if he is accepted at all. For there is none righteous, none able to merit his or her acceptance with God.

Whether any who have not heard the gospel will be accepted at the last by God we do not know. Our commission is clear: we are commanded to preach the gospel to every creature. See Genesis 18:25 and Matthew 28:19,20.

Every man has evidence of the existence of God
The Bible clearly indicates that every man in the world has enough evidence that God in fact does exist. Romans 1:19,20 tells us: 'For the truth about God is known instinctively (lit. is made known to them). God Himself has put this knowledge in their hearts. Since the earliest times men have seen the earth, sky and all that God has made. They have known of His existence and great eternal power. They will have no excuse—(when they stand before Him at the day of judgement). It is true some men say that there is no God but this is the unnatural results of continually denying His existence.'

Every man has also a moral standard within him
If a man is condemned, it is for violating God's moral standard within him. The revelation of that standard may be bright or dim, but every person in every society has within him a standard of some kind, and violation of that standard is sin. Romans 2:12-14 tells us that God will punish sin wherever it is found. He will punish the heathen when they sin, even though they never had

God's written laws, for down in their hearts they know right from wrong. God's laws are written in them; their own conscience accuses them, or excuses them if it is frequently ignored.

We see then that a man, even though he has never heard the gospel, can know (a) that God exists and (b) that he, the man, has failed to live as he ought. This knowledge comes through divine revelation and is of course the basis for man's 'religious search', which results in 'religion' as a way to God. Religion, however, is not the way to God—and never has been!

Questions for discussion at your group meeting:

What are some of the 'other religions' that you would be likely to meet as you go from door to door?

What are the basic tenets of these? Where are they wrong?

What different 'ways to God' do you think many people are trusting in today? (Some of these may not even be 'religious' at all.)

When you face your Maker, the issue will not be the heathen

Very often the question concerning what about the heathen is raised as a 'smoke screen' to avoid personal responsibility. We should answer the question as far as we can bearing in mind the three points stated above. The use of the Living New Testament version will be of help. We could then focus the issue on the person himself and ask; 'What will you do about Jesus Christ— you *have* heard about Him?' Read *The Case for Christianity* (C.S. Lewis) for a fuller discussion of this matter.

Jesus Christ affirmed that He was the only way to God

Our Lord was as clear as clear could be. He did not say He was a way, but the way. If we are faithful to Him, then we must take our stand upon what He says. We are dealing here with a revelation—God Himself has spoken by Jesus Christ; 'I am the Way, the Truth and the Life. No one can get to the Father except by means of Me.' (John 14:6). The apostle Peter said almost the same thing; 'In none other [than Jesus] is there salvation; for neither is there any other name . . . wherein we must be saved.' (Acts 4:12). The writer to the Hebrews evidently thought the same, for he said; 'How shall we escape if we neglect so great a salvation?' (Hebrew 2:3).

Neither sincerity nor intensity of faith can create truth. Faith is as valid as the object is valid in which it is placed. Believing a thing does not make it true, any more than refusing to believe it makes it false. The real issue is the question of what is truth.

Religions of the world are man's attempts to discover God and to enter into fellowship with Him. Christianity is the very opposite; it is the revelation of God to man in the person of Jesus Christ. The gulf between God and man cannot be bridged from man's side (religion) at all.

Christianity is unique in this respect; it is the revelation of God, 'who for us men and our salvation came down from heaven.' Read *Religion, Origin and Ideas* by Robert Brow (Tyndale).

Questions for discussion at your group meeting:

How would you answer the person who said: 'But surely Christ was being a bigot when He claimed to be equal with God?' or 'How do we know that He really made such a statement?' or 'Could He not have been under some kind of delusion of greatness?'

Group Bible Study No. 8: How Can We Explain the Miracles of the Bible?

Have you prayed first?

It is sometimes asked; 'How in this scientific age can a person who believes in the orderliness of the universe believe in miracles?'

Let us consider a few Bible related miracles:

Matt. 8:2,3,5-17, 24-27,28-32.

Matt. 9:2-8,18,20-22, 23-25.

Matt. 9:27-30,32-35.

Matt. 12:10-13,22.

Matt. 14:19-21,24-33, 35,36.

Matt. 15:21-28,32-39.

We can spend a lot of time, if we are not careful, discussing such matters as whether Christ walked on the water and whether He did feed the 5,000. Did the children of Israel really walk through the Red Sea, a wall of water standing up either side of them? Then what about the 'bigger' miracles? The virgin birth and the resurrection of Christ from the dead—did they really happen?

The real issue is, does an all powerful God exist or not? If we believe in an all powerful, all knowing and eternal God, who created the universe in the first place, then miracles cease to be incredible. Granted a God who is big enough to create and uphold the universe, then we accept that He can intervene in the universe He has called into being. The Christian answer to 'How can miracles be possible?' is simply: 'I believe in an Almighty God!'

Were people not more simple in New Testament times?
This is hardly true. People then were just as surprised as we would be now to see 5,000 being fed by five loaves or to see a man walking on the water. Mary, a virgin, was just as astonished as any girl would be today, when told she was going to have a baby outside the normal course of nature. Joseph at first jumped to the same conclusion as any man would today if his fiancee told him she was expecting a child and knowing that he was not responsible. The contemporaries of Jesus were credulous folk, prepared to believe anything. They said: 'Never since the world began has it been heard that a man opened the eyes of a man born blind'. Thomas affirmed: 'Except I see in His hands the print of the nails and place my fingers in the mark of the nails, and place my hand into His side, I will not believe'.
Questions for discussion at your group meeting:
What is the most difficult miracle in the Bible to believe? Why is it so difficult? How can we explain to a person who doubts the miracles that unbelief could be motivated by an unwillingness to face the moral challenge that belief would bring?

Scientific pronouncements do not explain why!
Boyle's law says: 'The volume of a given mass of gas is inversely proportional to the pressure upon it if the temperature remains constant'.
Now this law describes what regularly happens, but it does not explain why it happens or that it should always happen. As science progresses, we may break down existing laws into more basic units; in this case we may explain Boyle's law in terms of movement of molecules of gas, but this still does not explain why it happens, or

that it should always happen. We may progress even further and talk in terms of sub-atomic particles. Yet no matter how far we progress, we are still not explaining why it happens or that it always should.

Scientific laws never do express the ultimate cause for things behaving as they do. They only define what normally happens; they cannot affirm that things will always behave in that way. Also, some things just cannot be calculated by science. Who has ever measured a length of love or weighed a quantity of justice?

The ultimate miracle, the supreme credential, is the resurrection of our Lord Jesus Christ. If He was what He claimed to be then we should find no problem in believing all that the Bible says about Him. The resurrection has been called the best attested *fact* in history—a miracle if ever there was one!

Questions for discussion at your group meeting:

Concerning the resurrection of Christ, how would you answer a person who said: 'The body of Jesus was stolen by His disciples!' or 'Those who claimed to have seen Him, wanted to—a wish fulfilment!' or 'They went to the wrong tomb and of course the body was not there!'

Suggested further reading:

The Evidence for the Resurrection by Prof. N. Anderson (IVP);

Who Moved the Stone? by F. Morris (Faber);

You Must Be Joking by Michael Green (Hodder & Stoughton).

CHAPTER 4

Literature for Use
in Door to Door Visitation

It is because visitation evangelism has been generally neglected that there is a lack of good literature available, literature specially designed for this type of ministry. Many ministers and church leaders produce their own, which unfortunately is often poorly reproduced or based upon the wrong principles for effective door to door visitation.

In this chapter I am going to comment upon eight types of material which can be used in various forms of door to door visitation. At the end of each section I shall list the names and addresses of the societies or publishers who may be able to provide samples of the kind of literature with which the section deals. This will inevitably mean repeats of certain sources of literature under more than one section, but this will be more helpful, I think, than one list covering all types.

Scripture portions, books and Bibles

I am convinced that of all the different kinds of literature that we can use in door to door work, there is none better than the Word of God itself. It is true that in certain situations a particular tract or booklet might appeal to us as the most likely to be used of God, but overall the Word of God will be found to be most effective.

(a) Gospels

There are now very many versions, colours and sizes! The Bible Societies are constantly publishing new editions to meet different and changing requirements. It was good to see *Good News for the North by a man named Mark* produced especially for a united church visitation outreach to the North of England. This was one of the few occasions when the literature was designed with door to door visitation in view. There are, of course, many other types of Gospels, and it would be worthwhile to write to the various Bible Societies asking to see some of their latest publications.

There are Gospels designed to help the Christian workers, see for example, *The Marked New Testament* (Scripture Union); *The Gospel of John—Horton Edition* (Moody Press); *Peace Truth Love—the Living Gospel* (Pocket Testament League) and many others.

(b) *Portions of Scripture*

The Bible Societies are now publishing portions of Scripture to suit various seasons, types of people, ages and personal needs, for example, *The Christmas Story*, as told in the Gospel according to Luke. This booklet even contains the words, 'Greetings and best wishes for a Happy Christmas and New Year' inside the front cover. This kind of material can be very useful in door to door visitation during the Christmas season.

The Scripture Gift Mission have an excellent selection of booklets, containing just Scripture; daily readings like *Words of Comfort* or Bible based answers to problems, such as *For Your Need*. The latter is a booklet that every Christian interested in communicating should know well, especially door to door workers!

Having considered some of the latest publications of the various Bible Societies, using only the words of Scripture, many visitors will feel they need look no further as far as visitation literature is concerned. Why not write to the Societies listed and ask to see samples of their latest publications?

British and Foreign Bible Society, 146 Queen Victoria Street, London, EC4V 4BX.
Kingsway Publications, Lottbridge Drove, Eastbourne, Sussex.
Little Bible Ministry, 9 London Road, Bromley, Kent.
Moody Press, c/o 9 London Road, Bromley, Kent.
National Bible Society of Scotland, 5 St Andrew's Square, Edinburgh, EH9 2BL.
Pocket Testament League, 16 Holwood Road, Bromley, Kent.

Scripture Circulation Movement, 42 Fountainhall Road, Edinburgh, EH9 2LW.
Scripture Gift Mission, Eccleston Street, London SW1.
Scripture Union, 5 Wigmore Street, London W1.
Trinitarian Bible Society, 217 Kingston Road, London SW19 3NN.

Tracts and gospel booklets

The listing of tracts and gospel booklets is more difficult. There are tracts and booklets designed for all kinds of evangelistic opportunities, but, again, very few seem to have been designed with door to door visitation in view.

Because of growing interest more 'conversation-starter' tracts are now being printed. Years ago, the great point of a tract was that it should contain 'the whole counsel of God'. We then moved from the plain statement of gospel facts to the interest-awakening, story type of tract with a closing gospel thrust. More recently we have seen the rise of functional tracts that can be used in predetermined situations. Some tract societies are beginning to realise that there is need for bright, direct, even controversial cards, which make one main point, issue a challenge or call for a comment, for example, the snow scene (or was it a cloud formation?) that suddenly depicted the face of Christ, or the breathalyser test card which, if it did not change colour (it rarely did!), advised: 'Then you're fit enough to come to church next Sunday!'

Some tracts move straight in at common objection points, for example: *There Is No God!* (Concordia) would be very useful with certain types of visitation letters, also *Why Doesn't God Stop the Trouble?* (Victory Tract Club).

Why not write to some of the societies listed below, asking to see samples of what they have to offer, especially for door to door visitation?

Christian Literature Crusade, 201 Church Road, London SE19, 2PT.
Christian Publicity Organisation, Ivy Arch Road, Worthing, Sussex.

Drummond Tract Depot, Stirling, Scotland.

Evangelical Tract Society, 264 High Road, Harrow Weald, Middx.

Latimer Publishing Company, Capernwray Hall, Carnforth, Lancs.

Send The Light Trust, 9 London Road, Bromley, Kent.

Scripture Circulation Movement, 42 Fountainhall Road, Edinburgh, EH9 2LW.

Victory Tract Club, 189 Brighton Road, South Croydon, Surrey.

There are dozens of American tract societies, but one whose productions have often appealed to me personally is:

Concordia Tract Mission, Box 201 St. Louis, M.O., 63166, USA.

Magazine inserts, magazines and newspapers

Many of the magazines listed below are obtainable as inserts for the Parish (or church) Magazine, which if taken each month by a visitor make a useful reason for a regular contact with those who do not attend church. The content of these inserts varies considerably. Some are full of interesting and informative articles, but one looks in vain for such saving truth as would lead a reader to Christ! Others seem to be running on the same track so long, with so much saving truth, but there is little of real interest to the non-Christian. Obviously the kind of area in which the visitation is taking place must be considered to determine the magazine or newspaper to be used.

The wise visitor will be acquainted with the eight items listed below and will use his good sense as to which he would use, if any, in his visitation work.

The Sign and the Window, Alden and Mowbray Ltd., The Alden Press, Osney Mead, Oxford OX2 0EG.

Home Words, Ludgate Square, London EC4M 7AY. (I understand from the editor that this must remain entirely within the control of the Incumbent of each parish).

News Extra, Appleford, Abingdon, Berkshire.

Guideposts, The Witney Press, Marlborough Lane, Witney, Oxon.

This publication appears both as a monthly insert for

magazines and as a bi-monthly magazine complete in itself. A lady is selling the magazine *Guideposts* in Cornwall and her order at the time of writing is 1,000 per issue! The magazine looks attractive, is a convenient size and contains a nice balance of content with distinctive spiritual, take-away thought, with which readers can identify.

Message of Victory, 1 Library Street, Church, Accrington, Lancs.

This also appears as a magazine insert and as a magazine, undated, in its own right. It is suitable for door to door visitation.

Challenge Newspapers, Revenue Buildings, Chapel Road, Worthing, Sussex.

Challenge has been described as the key to open the doors in visitation work, doors into homes, and, more important, doors into hearts. *Challenge* is published each month in a form and language that is readily understood. People are glad to receive it and this makes the distributor a welcome visitor.

Method of approach

The most common method is to deliver copies of *Challenge* to a number of homes in a given area for a period of two or three months. This is then followed by a personal visit telling people you would like them to receive it regularly. Response varies widely, but the average seems to be about one in three. Some of these will be willing to pay for it; in the case of the elderly it can be offered free, payment being made by the local church as part of their evangelistic outreach. However many or few respond, the main thing is that the visitor is gaining access to somewhere there is a willingness to receive *Challenge*.

There is a lot to be said for selling the paper once folk have been given a number of free samples, but the cost of free distribution need not be a heavy financial burden, e.g. 20 people using in all 1,000 copies a month would need to subscribe about 15p a week each to cover the cost.

Letter in connection with Challenge

'Three of our [*Challenge*] readers have recently come to the Lord. Their first contact with the church was . . .

when they attended a special gathering of *Challenge* readers . . . Now they are members of the church and are themselves *Challenge* distributors.'   J.W.

'I had the joy of receiving the first convert to come into membership on a recent Sunday, who was contacted first through our *Challenge* distribution.'   C.T.

News Special is published six times a year (every other month). It can be used as a multiple tract in personal work or as a church outreach paper. It is undated and overprinting in the local news space can also be arranged.

Plus is for the 11-15 year olds. It is the only regular Christian comic-type material available for the young teens. These are both obtainable from the same address as *Challenge*.

Emergency Post. The Paternoster Press, Paternoster House, 3 Mount Radford Crescent, Exeter, Devon.
This little magazine has had an amazing ministry since October, 1939 when it first appeared. Its monthly circulation varies between 130,000 and 160,000. *Emergency Post* can also be used as a magazine insert; it costs only 2p per copy and can be a very effective method of making the message clear and plain.

Alive, Central Bible Hammond Trust Ltd, 50 Gray's Inn Road, London WC1X 8LT.
The building of a regular 'magazine round' using one of the above magazines or newspapers is a comparatively simple matter. The right magazine or paper must be chosen having regard to the area in which you are working—and the resources available. The visitor from the local Anglican church has a distinct advantage over the nonconformist. He can say: 'I am calling from the parish church,' and even if many do not attend the church, they sense a closer connection to it than any other and may be willing to subscribe to the parish magazine.

The problem, however, once the 'magazine round' has been established is to follow through the personal calls and to discover a way of communicating the good news of the gospel in greater depth. This will be the subject of our next chapter. It is very easy for the monthly call with the magazine or the newspaper to degenerate into a social contact and never become an evangelistic opportunity, apart from the literature being received.

Pre-visit letters

The subject of pre-visit letters has already been dealt with briefly in Chapter 3, but here we now want to deal with it in more detail.

There are not many societies or literature agencies at present who are producing for local use a ready printed or duplicated pre-visit letter. Most churches and fellowships these days have access to a duplicating machine or lithograph machine and the locally produced letter will probably have advantages over the mass-produced, can-be-used-anywhere type of letter.

There are, however, several agencies who supply headed paper, on which may be printed or duplicated your own pre-visit letter:

Bible Lands, P.O.Box 50, High Wycombe, Bucks.
Concordia, 117 Golden Lane, London EC1.
Christian Publicity Organisation, Ivy Arch Road, Worthing, Sussex.
The Fishers Fellowship, 96 Plaistow Lane, Bromley, Kent.

These agencies would send samples upon request.

The approach used in the letter

This can vary according to the area in which you are working, the interests of the local people and the good sense of the composers of the letter.

Some would prefer the almost flippant kind of approach, as used in the 'Call to the North' pre-visit leaflet:

'Those people from the church have been round again.
— Oh yes, what did they want this time?
— Nothing, they just left this bit of paper.
— And they'll want some money out of it, too, or else they'll have something to sign.
— Well, there is a coupon, but it seems to be giving something away.
— Don't you believe it! The church can't afford to

give things away today. They don't get enough in
the collections to give any back.
— But it says they'll drop a book in, if someone says
they'll read it . . .'

Then there is the more informative and direct approach, such as:

Dear Friend,
 During the next few weeks our church is to share in
a Visitation Mission to the district and we hope to have
the opportunity of visiting your home during the
course of the Mission. The purpose of our visit is two-
fold: first of all, to offer our friendship and help in any
way possible. Our other aim is of supreme importance:
we believe that God is concerned about all our lives
and has sent His Son, Jesus, to be our Saviour and
Friend. I am sure you will give our visitor a kindly welcome. If you are already a member of another church, I
trust you will not resent our calling. We do not desire
to take people from other churches, but are particularly anxious to be of help to those folk in our area who
have no firm contact at all . . .'

This letter (actually used in one area) you will notice
does extend an invitation to the church. We have already
seen that this is not one of the best initial approaches.
The offer to 'help' could also be laying the church open to
many situations it cannot cope with.
 Some visitors will feel that the pre-visit letters we have
so far considered are just not realistic enough. They are
rather like the fireman who goes to rescue a man from a
burning building and is asking: 'Would you be more
comfortable in an overcoat this cold weather or a raincoat
as I take you to safety?' The following kind of letter
would seem to be more to the point:

 'Do you think we are about to enter an age of peaceful existence? Did you know that 4,000 A-bombs can
demolish the earth and that Russia alone has 10,000 of
them? There are three ways in which the entire
world's population could be wiped out *in a few hours*!
The first is the hydrogen bomb, the second a deadly
toxin, and the third, nerve gases. Three ways of world

annihilation—just think of that! But who would want to destroy the world? Is it not a fact that mankind is becoming more peaceful, more humane, more reliable, truthful, loving and better in every way? Is it not a fact that the divorce rate is dropping, marriage vows are being honoured more, crime is decreasing and juvenile delinquency is becoming a thing of the past? No, these are not facts. Statistics reveal that wickedness and ungodliness are increasing on every hand. The Bible is right, after all, then, when it has been telling for years: 'In the last days, perilous times will come . . . etc.'

It will be seen from the foregoing that there are different types of approaches: some will appeal to some people, others to others. There can be no such thing as the ideal pre-visit letter, because the readers will be so different. You may find, however, the one reproduced in the third chapter of this manual can be adapted suitably for your local use.

The pull-away appeals of the letter
Again these will vary according to the purpose of the visit. A bad appeal would be 'Come to our church', a more effective one would be, 'We would appreciate your help'.

The objective of the letter must always be clearly borne in mind. It is to arouse interest, to encourage involvement and to prepare the person receiving it for an expected and even welcome visit.

It should be remembered that the letter can be delivered together with a leaflet, newspaper or magazine. In fact, reference to this literature could be made in the letter. We hesitate to mention specific items, but *There Is No God* (Concordia), *Why Doesn't God Stop the Trouble?* (VTC) and *The Incomparable Christ* (Scripture Circulation Movement) are particularly good examples of materials which could be included with the letter.

Appearance and production of the letter
Housewives today receive multitudes of letters advertising various commodities. Many of the 'free coupon' soap powder type have a similar look and feel about

them. It is not surprising that many busy people have a built-in resistance to them, instinctively recognise them and consign them to the waste bin. It is for this reason that many Christian communicators would recommend that we use duplicated letters rather than try to copy the colourful and glossy advertising of the commercial world.

Finally with regard to the pre-visit letter, consider the possibility of distributing a series of them before actually making the call. One church produced a series of six leaflets, which we here repeat for your interest and possible adaptation to your local situation. You will notice that once again the primary appeal seems to be 'Come and worship with us!'

Leaflet No. 1

> The Central Hall
> Invites you each Sunday to our family services, at 11.00 a.m. and 6.30 p.m.
> The friendly church.

Leaflet No. 2

> Have you forgotten we sent you an invitation to come and worship with us at
> The Central Hall?
> Do come and see us soon, a welcome awaits you every Sunday at 11 a.m. and 6.30 p.m.
> The friendly church.

Leaflet No. 3

> 'Knock, knock, who's there?'
> Was this the song of your choice?
> Actually, it is a most important question.
> Do you know the answer?
> Just as we keep knocking at your door, so the Lord Jesus Christ keeps knocking at the door of your life.
> Won't you open the door and let Him in?
> The friendly church.

(This third leaflet was distributed at the time of one of the European Song Contests).

Leaflet No. 4

> If your children are brought up at church it's not likely they will be brought up at court.

Why not send them to the Central Hall or better still bring them?
The friendly church.

Leaflet No. 5

If you are sick you call a doctor.
but if you are sick at heart, what then?
You would certainly find a friend to confide in at the Central Hall.
Perhaps we could help you.
The friendly church.

Leaflet No. 6

Yes! It's another leaflet from 'You know who' —The Central Hall.
You know our name now—we would like to know yours.
Come and join us and share our happy services on Sundays
11 a.m. and 6.30 p.m.
The friendly church.

It must be admitted that the recipient of these six leaflets would be assured of one thing at least—the Friendly Church, The Central Hall, would welcome him. But if he had not the time or the inclination to attend the church, little else is being achieved. The operation on the part of the leaflet distributors could hardly be called an evangelistic outreach.

From the information and the addresses given in this section it should be possible for your local visitation team prayerfully to compose a suitable pre-visit letter or letters to prepare the way for your visitation.

The simplest type of pre-visit leaflet I have seen was that produced in connection with Chippenham Council of Christian Churches Visitation, for which I had the privilege of providing the basic training of the workers and teaching of visitation principles. It was simply a medium notepaper-size leaflet, half of which was coloured mauve and contained a large black cross. The other half contained the words:

Chippenham Council of Christian Churches Visitation.
It is intended to call at the homes of all the people in your area. You will be visited in the near future. We

look forward to contacting you and offering any help we are able to give.

Here we have a simple, dignified leaflet, stating a call will be made and indicating an offer of help. One improvement to such a leaflet might be the request for the person visited to help us—rather than we help them!

The Christian survey

There are many ways of gaining contact with persons to share the gospel. Once the contact has been made, however, we face what is a real problem to many visitors, that of steering the conversation towards spiritual issues. Some prefer the direct or what might be called the 'shock' approach, others prefer to be more circuitous by discussing natural and topical subjects before approaching the spiritual.

There is perhaps no more simple method of starting to talk about spiritual things than by asking questions. In fact, this is the way in which many Christians could become more effective in their witness for the Lord, to learn the art of asking the right questions and then giving the person the time and opportunity of expressing his or her answer. Our Lord Jesus Christ, when on earth, was the master Teacher and His use of questions, if studied in the Gospel, will soon begin to reveal His method. The Gospels record over one hundred questions, e.g. Luke 2:49, John 1:38, John 2:4. The questions of Jesus were of various kinds, practical, personal, rhetorical, stimulating, definite, searching, simple, silencing, clear and brief. They would make a man think, they would secure information, express an emotion, follow up a story, recall the known, awaken the conscience, elicit faith, clarify the present situation, rebuke a criticism or settle once and for all another question! Questions may be asked which are of a challenging nature, such as, 'Which church do you attend?' or which are thought-provoking, such as, 'How relevant do you think Christianity is today?'

The advantages of a Christian survey

Attention immediately directed to spiritual issues with-

70

out embarrassment to either party. It is wise to make the first question one to which the majority of people will answer, 'Yes', for example, 'Do you believe that there is a God, a Creator, or some Higher Power responsible for this earth and universe?'

The questions on a survey should become more thought-provoking as they go on and can sometimes provide opportunities for frank discussion. Many people are not only willing but wanting to talk about spiritual issues, and the use of a questionnaire can be a helpful means of starting such conversation.

Some Christians have reservations about using such a survey. The argument seems to be that it is dishonest; but could it not also be dishonest to ask questions without using a printed survey? It all depends surely upon the attitude of those conducting the survey. It is true that a survey can be 'used' in the wrong sense as a means to an end when one is not really concerned about what people think at all. It is also true that the survey can be conducted with a genuine desire to make people think and to know what they think. It is for this reason that I always recommend that the results of the survey should be tabulated for all visitors to see and discuss after visitation ventures. Indeed, some of the people we visit we find want to know the results of the survey, which gives us a good reason for calling back and having further conversation.

Types of Christian survey
There are four basic types of survey which visitation team leaders bear in mind as they compile a survey for local use:-

(a)   A survey related to literature previously distributed, e.g. *Challenge*.

(b)   A survey starting on a topical note designed to encourage the person to think and possibly to talk about spiritual matters.

(c)   A survey designed to enlist a non-Christian in some kind of follow-through course, e.g. *Pre-conversion postal course*.

(d)   A survey designed to obtain information regarding children or young people in the homes who may like to know about activities the church has for them.

Results of Chippenham Council of Churches survey

The survey card simply listed the denominations and churches in the town, and the key questions were: 'To which church are you affiliated, if any?' 'Are you a practising or non-practising member?' Other questions included surname, address (normally completed without asking), number of adults in the family, number of children, whether the children attended Sunday School, whether the person spoken to would like a further visit.

It was interesting to discover that of the 1,100 people visited in one section of the town 115 requested further visits. Church affiliations were:-

Church of England	500	Baptist	24
Methodist	141	Congregational	27
Salvation Army	23	Not interested	289
Others	41	Roman Catholic	63

There are several different kinds of Christian Survey cards and leaflets:

The Lebanon Missionary Bible College, Berwick-on-Tweed, Northumberland, has a detailed 15-question Survey.

Campus for Christ Crusade, 105 London Road, Reading, Berks, RG1 5BY, has useful surveys for work among students and for door to door visitation.

National Young Life Campaign, 10 Fairfield West, Kingston-upon-Thames, Surrey, has a printed *Youth Questionnaire*, very useful for street evangelism.

The Fishers Fellowship, 96 Plaistow Lane, Bromley, Kent, also has all kinds of surveys and questionnaires. Why not write to the above and ask for samples of the kinds of questionnaire they have?

One of the most common failings in the do-it-yourself type of questionnaire for local use is that it is too long. It can be disconcerting to the person who opens the door to observe that the visitor has a foolscap sheet of questions, which he guesses is going to take at least half an hour to answer. The questions should be few, simple, open and to the point. Samples of surveys may be obtained from the Fishers Fellowship.

The visitation records

This is an aspect of door to door visitation in which it is easy to become too much taken up with details. We have seen some record cards which have been so complicated that the visitation workers need to take lessons on how they should be used! It may *seem* a good idea to have a complete dossier on the occupants and ages of a household, but apart from the difficulty of obtaining it and the greater difficulty of maintaining it, the *actual use* to which the information can be put does not warrant such detailed information being obtained.

The type of records kept will depend upon the use to which the information gained is put. There is no point in spending a lot of time otherwise.

Type of information generally considered useful
The names and address of the occupants, their approximate ages and the names and ages of the children; their church affiliation, if any, and whether regular in their attendance or not; their special needs, spiritual—to be taught the gospel and given an opportunity to respond, practical—to be helped in a material or advisory way; transport would be appreciated for them, being elderly, or for their children to the Sunday School; regular visits would or would not be appreciated; *Challenge* distributed each month, Parish or Church Magazine. Interest being shown in services, women's meeting, men's meeting, youth club, Sunday School, etc.

Some records contain spaces for dates of the first and subsequent visitors; spaces to record responses, profession, interests, hobbies, sports, etc. I think my reader will get my point. This whole subject of record-keeping can easily get out of hand and time be taken from our main mission, which is to communicate Christ.

Simplicity is the key note
All that is required is a supply of small record cards. A copy of the electoral roll can be purchased or copied from the local library. All you need to do is to ask for the particular Ward in which you are interested. It will cover many streets in a section of your district. At the top left-hand corner of a record card you print the name of the family in the home, followed by the initials of the house-

holder. At the top right-hand corner you print the number of the house and the road or street. The cards should be held together in sets of 10 or 15 by means of an elastic band, remembering to run the numbers either odds, or even, or as otherwise appropriate, so that 10 or 15 houses on the same side of the road will be visited. After each visit all the visitor needs to do is record the date of the visit, brief points of interest, which might help the next visitor, and a one, two or three star mark to indicate (1) Generally a friendly reception, (2) Interested—could call again, or (3) Very interested—should call again.

It is suggested that when the cards are returned they are filed away in appropriate street order; they are then ready for another consecutive visitation venture later on. A possible method is to file the cards in street order, but according to the star mark allotted. More experienced visitors could then be appointed to follow up the three-star contacts or the original visitors may prefer to undertake this, or the two and three-star contacts could be given personal invitations to home meetings or special services. Yet a third way is to begin to file the cards at this point in alphabetical order, which will mean that your consecutive visitation now become district visitation, but this needs to be watched carefully because district visitation can be so much more time consuming.

It is at this stage, following the initial visits to many homes that an effective and 'in depth' visitation programme will begin to emerge. The visitation, for whatever purpose or using whatever method, is undertaken in order to discover what may be called 'God-given contacts'. The main point of the record card is to provide a visible system by which God-given contacts are each followed through. The visitation team leaders will then begin to work out a strategy for the implementation of *evangelism*. Of course the visitor may have opportunity to evangelise at his first call, but it is generally conceded by experienced visitors that personal friendship must have been established first before effective communication is possible.

It is, in some ways, the easiest thing in the world to obtain 'friendly contacts', 'lonely souls', 'church-siders, but not church-attenders', any or all of whom may be God-given contacts. They will welcome the visitor when he calls. We must then be careful to see that the regular visit to that home does not become merely a social call and never an evangelistic opportunity. We are not saying there is no place for the purely social call, but normally we find among those who visit fairly regularly that their ministry has become just that, and nothing more. This is a 'weakness', if one may term it such, of many church leaders.

The use of sound records, tapes and cassettes

Although it is not literature, I am here including re-corded sound as a very important aid to door to door visitation work.

The Gospel Recordings Fellowship make available free of charge gospel messages on records in most of the languages in the world. These can be a very useful means of communication. In some of the homes to which we are invited, we discover those from other countries who would not object to our playing a record in their own language. Although there are a limited number available in English these include some helpful children's talks.

Gospel Recordings Fellowship,
Block 12E Gloucester Trading Estate,
Hucclecote, Gloucester, GL3 4AA.

The use of transistor tape recorders makes this kind of recorded ministry easier still today. There are many excellent tape-recording services, some containing hundreds of messages covering almost every topic imaginable. There will be a very wonderful field of evangelism opening up in this direction. Music is easy to obtain and it should not be difficult for visitation teams to produce a number of their own 10 or 15-minute home visitation programmes, which could consist of music, readings from Scripture and parts of messages. Many of the local radio programmes made by Radio World Wide could be adapted for this purpose. Such short tape re-cordings could be played in homes on a cassette recorder and could be the means of starting many a profitable discussion.

The following list will suggest sources of ministry and music, some which could be adapted or parts copied for making visitation tapes. The majority of the tapes available contain ministry for Christians, but most, if not all, will also have tapes suitable for non-Christians.

Back to the Bible Broadcasts, 18 Upper Redlands Road, Reading, Berks, RG1 5JR.

Bible Comes Alive, 3 Wisdom Court, Southcote Road, Reading, Berks.

Bible Teaching Tape Ministry, 25 Keswick Road, Boscombe, Bournemouth, BH5 1LP.

Birmingham Bible Institute Tapes, 6 Pakenham Road, Edgbaston, Birmingham, 15.

Calvary Radio Ministry Trust, 533a Chickerell Road, Weymouth, Dorset.

Chrissoure, Scotsburn, The Long Road, Rowledge, Farnham, Surrey.

Christian Recording Associates, 10 Downton Avenue, Streatham Hill, S.W.2.

Denis Clark Recordings, 100 Broadwater Street West, Worthing, Sussex.

East Midlands Outreach Organisation, 27 Beaconsfield Street, Long Eaton, Nottingham, NG10 1AY.

Evangelical Tapes Outreach, 1a Warren Gardens, Lisburn, Co. Antrim, Ireland.

Fishers Fellowship, 96 Plaistow Lane, Bromley, Kent, BR1 3AS.

Fountain Trust Library, Central Hall, Durnsford Road, London, SE1 8ED.

Gospel Tape Centre, Deodar, Lower Road, Hockley, Essex.

Independent Methodist Youth Department, 24 Percy Street, Nelson, Lancs, BB9 0AA.

Keswick Convention Tape Library, 13 Lismore Road, Eastbourne, Sussex.

New Life Recordings Trust, 40 Fairfield Road, Barton-on-Sea, Hants.

Prophetic Witness Recordings, 2 Upperton Gardens, Eastbourne, Sussex.

Send The Light Trust, 9 London Road, Bromley, Kent.

Shepherd Recordings, 2 Gloucester Close, Chippenham, Wilts.

St. Helens Tape Library, Gret Street, St. Helens, London, E.C.3.

Things that Matter, 30 Western Road, Flixton, Urmston, Manchester, M31 3LF.

Truth Tapes, 48 Queens Road, Ashford, Kent.

Vanguard Music Ltd., Gloucester House, 19 Charing Cross Road, London, W.C.2.

Voice of Life, 4 Albion Place, Maidstone, Kent.

The Voice of Life is a Christian supply service for short-wave radios and cassette tape recorders.

I have listed only 24 Christian recording libraries; there are probably many more. Most of these listed have over 100 recordings, and one or two at least over 1,000. The tapes and cassettes available include ministry, gospel messages, Bible readings, testimonies, music, children's talks and answers to common problems. One or two of your local visitation team could render a valuable service by hearing and sifting out parts of messages, musical items and testimonies thereby making a number of short programmes which could be played on cassette recorders by the visitors in the homes of the people. This whole area is one of great potential to evangelism and may provide one of the answers to the problem of turning a social visit into an evangelistic opportunity. We should be very interested to receive copies of such programmes in the Fishers Fellowship which we could loan to others working in this field.

With the large amount of material available, do not fail to include the plain reading of the Word of God itself, possibly in a modern version, and by a well-known personality.

Narrative portions of the Scripture, read by a number of different voices, can be very effective. It will be found that the Word of God can often get through to more people than a 'second-hand' message from a man. The Scripture Gift Mission booklet, *For Your Need*, or the Scripture Union daily Bible reading book, *Every Day*, could be utilised for such Scripture programmes.

Locally produced literature

In visitation evangelism there is a proper place for locally produced materials and literature. Obviously there is no need to produce locally Scripture portions, gospels, tracts, booklets, magazines and newspapers (sections 1, 2 and 3 in this chapter have suggested sources of these). Pre-visit letters, surveys, records and tape recordings are generally best produced locally. There will no doubt be many more printed pre-visit letters, intended for different areas, produced by various literature suppliers in the near future.

Yet another way you can find help in the production of a local pre-visit letter is to overprint (or duplicate) your own letter on a ready printed letterhead. We have good supplies of three of these in the Fisher Fellowship office at the present time, one beginning *What now?*, another '*We have our problems*' and the third '*Challenge*'. These can be ordered from the Fellowship at only a nominal charge per ream; samples of all three will be sent upon request.

If we find, as we expect, that such pre-printed letterheads are meeting a need, we will gladly feed in ideas to literature societies prepared to take on this service. There is no reason why we should not have a dozen or more such 'letterheads' to choose from on which local visitors can print or duplicate their own pre-visit letter.

Christian surveys and visitations records are also available from the literature suppliers (see section 5 and 6) but these, too, may be printed or duplicated locally. The temptation to make these too complicated or lengthy should be resisted. Simplicity and brevity are important for both locally produced surveys and records.

It is amazing what can be done with a duplicator. The Rev. Nigel Stowe, The Vicarage, St. Judes, Mildmay Park, London, N.1, has produced an excellent series of visitation hand-outs, magazines for the unchurched and thought-provoking innovations. Many of these have been duplicated on Concordia programme covers and letter-headings, and a colour catalogue entitled *To Live Is Christ* can be obtained from Concordia House Ltd., 117/123 Golden Lane, London, EC1Y 0TL.

If you are thinking of over-printing or duplicating leaf-lets write to Christian Publicity Organisation, Ivy Arch Road, Worthing, Sussex, asking for samples. A useful book on church publicity and contact material is *Loud and Clear* by John Capon, Falcon Press.

Regarding visitation materials and leaflets, it is best to make up your own Visitation Packs. Decide on the kind of material your visitors are to use, and then have a working party spend part of an evening making up packs of the materials ready for the visitors. It can be very disheartening to give a visitor, for example, 100 survey cards, 100 pre-visit letters, some gospel and other communication material with information on two or three streets you want him to cover. It will be found far better to place in suitable envelopes the materials required for ten visits only, i.e. ten pre-visit letters, then, assuming the survey method is being used, ten survey cards, a gospel or two for the very interested, and one or two 'bridge of life illustrations' (*The Little Green Book*, VTC).

Instructions could be duplicated on sheets and pasted on each pack—or it may be possible to duplicate direct on the envelope before they are prepared. Although it may take an extra evening to prepare a number of packs of material, you will find it far more convenient when it comes to the preparation of the workers and asking them to take a pack each. Those who wish to work in pairs may do so, but should use two packs between them. Ten may seem a small number to those unused to visiting in the 'contact making' way we describe in this manual. You will find, however, that two packs will contain adequate material for two workers for a week, unless they happen to have far more time available than is usual for church members. One assumes that with normal church meetings and other commitments only one evening will be devoted to visiting—the evening most convenient to both workers. By the time they have finished their daily work, had a meal, met to pray together to ask the Lord to make their way prosperous, the actual visiting will start between 7.30 and 8 p.m. and should not be extended much beyond 9 p.m. Allowing for time to reach the visitation area and return, barely an hour is left, in which the 20 visits may well prove far too many! When considered in this way, it will be seen that the 10-visit pack is not so small after all. In any event, it is far better to start with this number and increase it to say fifteen or twenty if it is found insufficient for an evening's visitation. It will depend partly upon your attitude to visitation work. If you have in mind covering as large a number of homes as possible, you will be less inclined to linger and talk with people. If, on the other hand, you have in mind making more worthwhile contacts for the Lord, each visit will be undertaken with special care, prayer, and without any sense of hurry. I am of the opinion that although there is undoubtedly some place for the more rapid method, the unhurried method is usually better.

Group Bible Study No. 9: Does Evolution Disprove the Genesis Account?

Have you prayed first?

Since the nineteenth century, one of the most popular objections to the early chapters of Genesis is the supposed conflict with the teaching of evolution. The Darwin theory suggests that each distinct type of living creation evolved from a simpler predecessor. Instead of separate creation of each distinct species, all species had a common origin. While we do not suggest the Christian visitors should make an issue of this point, they should be clear in their own mind that evolution is only a theory, not a proven fact, and that many believing scientists reject it as a theory as may be seen by reference to a book such as *Darwin, Evolution and Creation*, edited by Paul Zimmerman, Concordia.

Read chapter 1 of Genesis and make a list of God's works in order for each day. In what way was man made in God's image? How does man differ in kind, not merely in degree, from other creatures?

In what way did our Lord accept the Genesis account? Matthew 19:4.

In what way did Paul accept the Genesis account? 1 Corinthians 15:22,45.

Was Adam a real person or was he not? Romans 5.

Either we accept the teaching of the book of Genesis, or we accept one of the several theories of evolution. If told by a person we are visiting, 'But I cannot accept the Bible account of creation, I believe the theory of evolution', it may be sensible to ask, 'To which particular theory of it do you subscribe?'

Comparative anatomy

Similarity between man and the ape is still regarded as a major piece of evidence for evolution, in spite of the fact that some evolutionists now deny that man descended from the ape, and that both descended from some other creature. The argument is that the skeletons of men, gorillas, chimpanzees, orangoutangs and gibbons all show similar structures and therefore must be related to a common ancestor, if not to each other. The similarities however could just as well point to a common designer who used certain basic structures as best for certain purposes. There are also great differences which have yet to be explained; the mental gulf, the moral conscience, the ability to speak, differences in bone structure and only man walks upright on two legs.

The Bible says 'God created man in His own image, in the image of God He created him, male and female He created them'. Genesis 1:27. Concerning the way in which this was done we read; 'The Lord God formed man of the dust from the ground, and breathed into his nostrils the breath of life; and man became a living soul. . . .' Genesis 2:7.

Those who accept the theories of evolution disagree on many things, but on one thing they all agree—it was not done this way!

Either we believe God's Word and revelation by faith, or we accept man's supposition and changing speculations. Some Christians believe it is possible to accept both. What is your opinion and why—be ready to discuss this at your group meeting.

Embryonic recapitulation

Years ago this particular evidence of evolution was more popular than it is today. It was assumed and, incidentally, is still taught in many text books, that the human embryo passed through the various stages that occurred in the evolutionary history of the human race. Eager imaginations fancied that 'gill slits' were a recapitulation of the gill slits in a fish; but further investigation began to cast serious doubts on this particular evidence.

Several investigators have affirmed the doubtful evidence of embryonic recapitulation, including: Sir Gavin Beer, Prof. Waldo Shumway, Prof. John P. Van Haitsma, Prof. John W. Klotz, Prof. Philip G. Fothergill, Prof. W. R. Breeman, Dr. G. Stanley Hall and Dr. J. W. Simmons.

Read chapter 2 of Genesis and make a summary of man's early setting (verses 1 to 6). Then notice in verse 7 how a man was formed and how man became a living being. Some who accept both evolution and the Genesis account say 'man' here means 'mankind', i.e. all men; but see verses 18 to 25.

The record of the fossils

Fossils are the remains or traces of things that lived ages ago. They lie at various levels, much like the layers of a cake. How old are they? Since the beginning of the twentieth century scientists have been using radioactive methods for dating fossils. The evolutionist claims that because he can point to a fossil record it suggests change in development over a period of time. But does it? There are several missing chapters in the record of the rocks.

It should be possible to discover life forms dating back to the earliest geological periods. Instead the fossil record shows no life forms until the Cambrian period. The so-called Cambrian explosion began with at least nine or ten different forms of life. They have found evidence of some life forms before this, algae and certain kinds of worms, but not the traditional and expected 'missing links' each showing slight variations between the species.

If evolution were true then why is it not taking place today? In answer to these questions we are told that we have to cast our mind back to millions of years ago. We must not judge by present appearances, that is, do not be a scientist. We must use our imagination, and some have. In 1937 the third molar tooth of a fossil ape (they named it 'australopithecus transvaalentis') was triumphantly hailed by scientists all over the world as indicating man's direct descent from the ape. Now, many would deny this.

Further reading

Evolution,
   International Christian Crusade.
The Christian View of Science and Scripture,
   Bernard Ramm, Paternoster Press.
Scientific Creationism,
   Henry Morris, Creation Life, Send The Light Trust.
Man's Origin, Man's Destiny,
   A. E. Wilder Smith, Harold Shaw.
Creation or Evolution,
   Ron Smith, Fishers Fellowship.

Helpful cassette tapes
There is an interesting series of cassette tapes entitled
The Bible and Science, Dr. John Whitcomb, Jr.
   No. 4 of the series deals with Genesis and evolution.
   No. 5 deals with the origin of man.
Send The Light Trust, 9 London Road, Bromley, Kent.

Group Bible Study No. 10: Is Christian Conversion Only Psychological?

Have you prayed first?

   Questions which are sometimes asked of a Christian
are, 'But isn't your Christian experience of conversion
only a psychological change?' 'Why are you a Christian?
It is not because you recognised some kind of "good"
would come out of it, or you were brought up to believe in
Christ!'

Conditioning by childhood circumstances
Some people suggest we have faith only because we have
been conditioned since our childhood days to this 'way of
thinking'. Anyone who has travelled at all and met many
Christians will know that this over-simplifies the facts.
Christians have come to Christ from every imaginable
background. True some are raised within Christian families, but there are thousands who had no contact at all
with Christianity in their childhood. Consider Acts 9:1-9.
Visualise the tremendous change in Saul (See Acts 7:58
to 8:3). List his 'before' and 'after' characteristics. In
what circumstances did Jesus Christ confront you? Can

you recall others, whether in the Bible or out of it, who, like Paul, were not brought up in the Christian faith? (Matthew 4:21,11; Mark 5:1-8; Luke 19:1-6). Also there are many who were conditioned to the faith from childhood but now, sadly, have no personal faith in Christ at all. You may like to discuss in your group why this happens.

Conditioning by personal gain
Some will tell us that we have come to faith in Christ because of some personal gain or advantage such faith gives us. They assert that ideas of spiritual reality are essentially 'wish fulfilments'. All religious experiences, they contend, can be traced back to man's unconscious mind feeling a need for God. Man creates a mental image and then worships this mental projection. It is true of course that there is personal gain to be obtained through faith in Christ, peace with God, sins forgiven, co-operation in a divine purpose for the life, but these are often accompanied by personal loss, suffering, rejection, division within families, self-imposed restraints and submission to the will of another (Acts 6:8,10,15; 7:51-60; 16:19-24; 2 Corinthians 11:22-30). We sometimes hear it said, too, that religion is a kind of crutch for those who cannot get along in life alone. In cases this may be so but the history of the Christian Church, with its social reformers and martyrs for Christ, many of whom were outstanding personalities, proves that this view is a limited one. There is also a proper sense in which our faith is intended to be a means of strength greater than our own. (*Runaway World*, by Michael Green, IVP, is an excellent book to answer the 'mental crutch' idea).

How to know if we have been conditioned to believe
If our spiritual experience is merely a wish fulfilment, then we should be able to regard any object as God, an organ, for example. If we think of an organ as God long enough, then it will become 'God' to us and we may have an experience which we attribute to our 'God'! A man could say, for example, 'This organ is the greatest! I get joy, peace, satisfaction and purpose in life from it.' Well, now, we cannot argue with his personal experience but we can investigate it by asking him several ques-

tions. 'How do you know it is the organ that gives you these blessings?' 'Is there anybody else you know who found the same blessing through that same organ?' 'To what objective fact is your subjective faith tied?' It is just here that Christianity differs from all other psychological phenomena. The *Christian's* subjective experience is tied to the objective facts concerning a person, Jesus Christ—His virgin birth, His sinless life, His divine sonship, His substitutionary death and His glorious resurrection.

In many respects the person who accepts Christ is choosing the most difficult way of life. Conversion to Jesus Christ involves renunciation of self and continued trust and obedience in and to another. The true Christian today is still in the minority, still regarded as the odd man out, still opposed, persecuted and, in some places of the world, tortured for his faith in the Lord Jesus Christ.

The fact that Jesus Christ rose from the dead means nothing to me personally until I receive him as Saviour and Lord. The true Christian's experience of his day to day walk with Christ is based upon the solid objective facts in history concerning Christ, one of the greatest attested facts being His resurrection from the dead. Write out three reasons why you can logically 'believe' in the resurrection. Be ready to share these at your group meeting.

Consider 1 Corinthians 15:1-4. List exactly to whom He appeared. Who was saying there is no resurrection? What would have been the results if Christ had not been raised from the dead? Are you trusting Him for all He claimed to be and to do?

Further reading on the subject

Evidence for the Resurrection,
    J. N. D. Anderson, IVP.
Who Moved the Stone?
    F. Morris, Faber.
World Aflame,
    Billy Graham, World's Work.

Group Bible Study No. 11: A Morally Good Life Will be Accepted by God

Have you prayed first?

Ever since Cain offered the produce of the earth, the labour of his hands, rather than the provision of God, a sacrificial offering, man has tried to find acceptance with God by how he lives or what he does. To verify this ask some friends in your daily walk of life—how they expect to be accounted right before God. See Genesis 4:1-5. Why was Cain's offering rejected? What does 'sin lieth at the door' mean? (v.7). True a non-Christian can live a moral life and do good, but his life and works can never of themselves reach the standard required of God, if acceptance is to be gained that way. God's standard is *perfection* and this none has attained except Jesus Christ. No man dare claim: 'I have never done anything wrong or offensive to God; I am perfect!'

Good works in order to earn salvation is the average man's concept of religion. He imagines that the good works he does are somehow balanced against the bad works. The better kind of person he is, the more chance he has of gaining acceptance with God. He can often think of several who are not so moral as himself, and some with whom he might be compared as a saint! Most people will be found to accept this basic philosophy that, if we do our best, then everything will probably be all right in the end. What would you say to a person who speaks like this? Be prepared to share your answer at the next group meeting.

If we accept the teaching of the Bible, however, it is possible to be a 'good man' but lost (Acts 10:1,2). What else did this good man need?

All have sinned
Everyone is a sinner. 'All have sinned and come short of the glory of God' (Romans 3:23). The virgin Mary, the Pope, your minister, your elders, your mother, your father, you and I *all* have sinned. 'For there is not a just man upon the earth, that doeth good and sinneth not . . ' (Ecclesiastes 7:20). If you happen to know that the person you are visiting is very moral, then with sincerity compliment him, but with concern point out that he is not *perfect* in the sight of God (Isaiah 64:6; James 2:10).

Salvation only through faith
Nothing a man can *do* will help him to attain the perfec-

tion that God requires. 'For by grace are you saved through faith; and that not of yourselves; it is the gift of God, not of works lest any man should boast.' (Ephesians 2:8,9). 'But to him that worketh not, but believeth on Him that justifieth the ungodly, his faith is counted for righteousness' (Romans 4:5). 'Knowing that a man is not justified—that is made right with God—by the works of the law, but by the faith of Jesus Christ, even as we have believed in Jesus Christ, that we might be justified by the faith of Christ and not by the works of the law, for by the works of the law shall no flesh be justified' (Galatians 2:16). If anything at all is clear in Scripture, it is that a man is justified by faith in Christ—plus nothing!

These are key verses that every door to door visitor should know by heart. If a person implies that he is trusting in himself for salvation, then show him a passage like Ephesians 2:8,9 and stay with it. Ask him: 'How would you take those words "not of works"?' Some people are unwilling to accept what the Word says; this we know is calling God a liar and is very serious. How would you answer a person who says: 'But I do believe in Jesus *and* I do the best I can to get to heaven.' Be prepared to discuss this at your group meeting.

God has made Him (Jesus Christ) to be sin for us
Christ has made complete and final payment for all sin and offers His righteousness. 'For He [God] has made Him [Christ] to be sin for us, who knew no sin; that we might be made the righteousness of God in Him' (2 Corinthians 5:21). Christ never sinned. He alone lived a perfect life and fulfilled every standard. He took our sins upon Himself and suffered their judgment. He did this, not only that our sins should not be accounted to us, but that His righteousness and standing before God might also be ours. See Isaiah 53:6; 1 Peter 3:18; Colossians 2:13,14; Acts 13:38,39.

How would you answer a person who says: 'But to gain acceptance with God through the good works of another is morally unjust' (John 3:16; 10:17,18).

Having these great truths so clearly revealed, in your own mind, you can explain to the 'good person', 'Good though you may be, you are not good enough. You cannot receive eternal life by working for it or trying to improve yourself. You receive eternal life and acceptance with God by *believing* the record that God has given us concerning His Son, our Lord Jesus Christ.'

We should clearly understand that it is not that God has no regard to a man's good works, but that they cannot secure his salvation. The good works that God desires are those which are the fruit of salvation.

'This is the record, that God hath given to us eternal life and this life is in His Son. He that hath the Son hath life and he that hath not the Son of God hath not life.'

1 John 5:11,12.

CHAPTER 5

Problems, Difficulties and Excuses

In visitation evangelism, as with most forms of evangelism, we shall meet those who have barriers to belief, problems they would like the Christian to answer and difficulties which may or may not arise from honest doubts. In many cases the problems raised, whether biblical, scientific or philosophical, are of a justifying nature: they do not arise from a desire to believe, but a desire to doubt.

Divine truth always carries with it a normal challenge and those who are willing to believe recognise instinctively that they must be prepared to act. It is therefore more often an unwillingness to believe, rather than an inability to believe, that we have to contend with (Matthew 23:37; John 5:39,40). How can we tell whether a man is unwilling to believe or unable? Discuss this question at your group meeting.

How should we help those with problems?

First, we ought to pray for them. Their basic need is conversion. It is by prayer that we can prepare for the Holy Spirit to do the work that only He can do—to convict of sin, righteousness and judgment. We have known those who have had seemingly endless problems; as soon as one has been answered, another is brought forward. But when that person has been truly convicted of his need of Christ the problems have not then seemed so important.

Then there are the sincere doubters, who in their more thoughtful moments would like to believe. They realise that unbelief gives no real peace to their hearts and solves few problems to their intellectual satisfaction. More than one non-Christian has been heard to say to a

Christian: 'I would give anything to believe as you do and to live the kind of life you live!'

Secondly, we must share with them, if we know it, the Christian answer to their problems. If we do not know it, we must of course be honest and admit it, but say that we will try to discover the Christian answer and ask whether we may call again to explain it. Never call a person a dishonest doubter, as this would be to sit in judgment upon his sincerity. On the other hand, we must not be so naive as to give him the impression that a Christian and a simpleton are one and the same.

The Bible, in this as in other matters of faith and practice, has the perfect answer, which is in two parts: (a) 'When arguing with a rebel, don't use foolish arguments as he does, or you will become as foolish as he is!' (b) 'Prick his conceit with silly replies'! (Proverbs 26: 4,5).

In other words, there is a time to be serious, particularly as you convey divine truth; but if the other person is obviously not serious, there is little point in your being so. Therefore answer a fool 'as his folly deserves', as one translation has it. A serious reply to a light remark can, however, sometimes redirect a conversation into a sensible path.

Some Christians make the mistake of allowing themselves too easily to be drawn into argument. They become flustered and even express anger. They have yet to learn this is not 'the way the Master went'. Quietly commit yourself to Christ your Lord and if anybody asks you why you believe as you do, be ready to tell him, but do it in a gentle and respectful way.

The Christian visitor should always keep his motives pure. Argument for its own sake is never profitable; but if the purpose is to reason the truth in order to show the relevance of Christ, then it may be helpful to reason with a person. Do not think, however, that you can reason a person into regeneration. This would be to usurp the work of the Holy Spirit. Such 'conversions', and there are some, are about as real and lasting as some of those wrought through emotional appeals; neither can be truly spiritual without the simultaneous action of the Spirit of God in cleansing the heart and imparting new life.

The honest doubter

The honest doubter is a person with a real intellectual difficulty who is willing to have it resolved. He is not far from the kingdom and having encountered a real Christian he will be willing to investigate truth in every reasonable way suggested. He may try to solve his problems by mere intellectual reason, but he will find that eventually he reaches a position where reason indicates two ways, the way of faith and the way of unbelief. Jesus said: 'My teaching is not mine, but His that sent Me. If any man is willing to do His will, he shall know of the teaching, whether it is of God, or whether I speak from Myself' (John 7:17). If your friend is really honest, he will be willing to 'test' the way of faith. How can such a test be made? What is God's will in this connection? It is that a man should pray for light, repent of his sin and believe in Christ. Here then is a method of serious research that an honest doubter will not decline to follow. Really determine to do the will of God and assurance as to Christ's teaching will soon follow.

Another simple suggestion to the honest doubter, one who says that he would be willing to believe, is to give him a copy of John's Gospel, and ask him to pray for God's help as he reads a chapter each day. In our door to door visitation we shall meet many people who will respond to a challenge of this kind.

The dishonest doubter

There are several types of these. The Infidel is the avowed unbeliever. The Secularist is the doubter who cares only for the present life. The Humanist rejects God and cares only for man. Then there is the Rationalist who claims that human reason is the final court of appeal. Finally we have the Liberalist; he may have some degree of religious belief but rejects the plain view of the Bible with its offer of salvation through faith in Christ.

Bearing in mind the biblical advice about answering a person according to his disposition of mind, the Christian visitor should be prepared to spend time in personal preparation in one of the most common areas of unbelief.

In the main there are three categories into which most of the problems we face can be placed:

(a) Problems concerning the Bible, inspiration and the supposed difficulties or contradictions in the Bible.

(b) Problems concerning the origin of man, the theory of evolution and other scientific issues which may seem incompatible with belief.

(c) Problems concerning other religions in the world, how they compare with the Christian faith, and deviations from the historic biblical faith.

We find, as might be expected, that there are an abundance of booklets and books dealing with these basic problems. It is good for Christians to 'do their homework' and to understand some of the basic issues involved and the Christian answer.

Bible inspiration and Bible difficulties

There are many excellent books which one should read and study to be well informed in this field. Regarding Bible inspiration, for example, one could scarcely find a better booklet than *The Inspiration of the Scriptures*, Loraine Boettner (The Christian Book Depot, Bristol). Then to read *Fundamentalism and the Word of God*, J. Packer (IVP), will certainly strengthen one's faith in the inspired Word that God has caused to be written for our learning.

We now turn to the more common Bible difficulties in the form in which they are stated by the ordinary man. 'Where did Cain get his wife from?' 'What about the mistakes in the Bible?' Now two most helpful paperbacks which between them cover almost every problem of this nature we can meet are *Difficulties in the Bible*, R.A. Torrey (Moody Press) and *Bible Difficulties*, W. Arnt (Concordia).

Nearly 100 of these common problems, difficulties and excuses related to the Bible are clearly answered in these two books. Many problems have been answered in great detail by men who have investigated their subject fully. The question has often been asked, for example: 'Was there really a flood?' I have a book of 374 pages in my library, *The Flood in the Light of the Bible, Geology and Archaeology*, A.M. Rehwinkel (Concordia).

Evolution and science

Here again we consider a field rich in books and booklets which set out biblical viewpoints and correct non-biblical ones. Evolution, for example, is regularly taught in schools, colleges and universities and, apart from a minority voice from believing creationists, no other view is upheld. A number (some would say a growing number) of practising Christians who are also scientists are rejecting evolutionary theories and accept by faith the creationist viewpoint. There is in some quarters a tendency to ignore this particular issue and to confess agnosticism concerning it because of admitted lack of scientific training. The fact of the matter is that there are those who have been scientifically trained and still do not accept the theory of evolution. There is a useful little booklet called, *Evolution, Science Falsely So-called* (International Christian Crusade). This booklet has now run into 18 editions; every year it is revised and brought up to date with the latest findings. This is more than can be said for many of the text books being used to teach evolution in our schools and colleges at the present time. Then from the USA there is *Evolution on Trial* by Cora Reno, B.Sc. (in Zoology), M.A. (in Zoology) and Ph.D. at the University of California. Her earlier publication, *Evolution, Fact or Theory?* has sold over 200,000 copies (Moody Bible Institute).

If Christian workers want a little more mind-stretching in this field, then *Darwin, Evolution and Creation*, Paul A. Zimmerman, editor (Concordia) or *Man's Origin, Man's Destiny*, A.E. Wilder Smith (Harold Shaw), can help. A more popular presentation of the creationist viewpoint will be found in *The Early Earth*, John Whitcomb (Baker Book House).

Those who would like to consider how other scientists, who are also Christians, evaluate and hold to certain aspects of evolution, are recommended *The Christian View of Science and Scriptures*, Bernard Ramm (Paternoster Press). There are dozens of books and booklets now available in this field of origins and of scientific speculation in contrast with simple belief in the Bible. It will help some visitors, particularly those who have a special interest in such scientific issues, to read some of the books quoted in this section, and to be reminded that evolution is not so obviously the fact it is often assumed to be. We do not need to get involved in scientific discussions in our visitation work in the normal way. In my experience we are encountering more non-Christians than ever who are questioning evolution, while those who affirm it is true and therefore the Genesis account is not to be trusted can be reminded, evolution is still yet, but a theory!

Religions of the world and deviations from historic Christianity

The argument in its simplest form is that, seeing there are so many religions (and some older than Christianity), they cannot all be right, so how do you know that Christianity is the right or the only true one? First, let us think about the major religions of the world. They will often be found listed in the back of old Bibles, and some of the accompanying articles give helpful suggestions for speaking to those of other faiths.

There are very few books which describe the major religions of the world and suggest how we can best communicate to those who follow them. One recent booklet is *Asians in Britain*, Patrick Sookhdeo (Paternoster Press). Another is *So What's the Difference?*, a biblical comparison of true Christianity with four major religions and four major cults, edited by Fritz Ridenour (Gospel Light Publications). *Christianity and Comparative Religions*, J.N.D. Anderson (Tyndale Press), and *Christianity Amid the Great Religions*, N. Smart (SPCK) are two other instructive books. Also, the Edinburgh House Press have a useful series entitled: *The Christian Approach to the Muslim*, *The Christian Approach to the Buddhist*, etc.

Turning then to deviations from the historic Christian faith, two helpful but similar books are: *Cults and Isms*, J. Oswald Sanders (MMS), and *Other Gospels*, Paul B. Smith (MMS). For those who desire to make a more comprehensive study of the cults, *The Kingdom of the Cults*, Walter R. Martin (Bethany Fellowship) is the kind of volume they would find informative.

In visitation work, we shall obviously encounter Roman Catholics. Some will be found to be very devout and regular in church attendance; others will use their past association with the Roman Catholic Church as an excuse for not continuing in conversation. When asked if they now attend church, they are soon discovered to be 'Roman Catholics' in name only. The same may be said of those who confess allegiance to other communions. In visiting, therefore, we should always try to discover how deep is their actual relationship to the church they profess, but then more important how deep it is to our Lord Jesus Christ. Of course we shall meet Roman Catholics who love Christ, are truly born again of the Holy Spirit, and whose daily devotional life would shame us. It is well, however, especially necessary in areas where they will encounter many Roman Catholics, for visitors to know what Roman Catholics believe and why non-Catholics hold different opinions. Our differences are caused by reason of the fact that we are accepting different sources of authority for our faith. The evangelical Christian accepts the Word of God, and that alone, as his rule of faith and conduct, and believes that in the Bible are all things necessary for faith in order to find acceptance with God.

The Roman Catholic, however, is required to accept a threefold source of authority: (a) the Bible, (b) the Church Fathers and (c) the ex cathedra pronouncements made by the Pope, that is, seated in his papal chair, the 'chair of Peter' and speaking in his official capacity as 'head of the church'. *Leading Roman Catholics to Christ*, Wilson Ewin (Christian Publications Centre), is helpful, but a little harsh in parts, one feels, towards the Roman Catholic Church. (Truth and grace, however, always have been difficult to hold in balance). *Roman Catholicism*, Loraine Boettner (Banner of Truth), provides a very comprehensive and up-to-date survey of the teaching and practices of the Roman Church—all 600 pages but one of it!

In visitation we encounter communists, too, sometimes very ardent communists. On the factory floor also the Christian will find himself faced with the question of communism. This philosophy of dialectical materialism often gives its adherents the drive to attempt to change the world in accordance with its teaching. It is for this reason that it is considered to be one of the world's foremost religions by some. *Communism and the Christian Faith*, Robert Schaplemann (Concordia), is only a 38-page booklet and a fuller treatment of this subject will be found in *The Christian Answer to Communism*, Thomas O. Kay (Zondervan). These publications will be found to provide some telling answers to a number of the questions posed by communists.

There is an increasing interest also in psychic research, parapsychology, extra sensory perception, spiritism, witchcraft and Satan worship. Already many books have appeared on these and allied subjects. This whole realm of the occult is becoming extremely popular and we have no doubt that it will become more so as the end of the age approaches. Visitation workers would be informed by reading *The Fortune Sellers*, Gary Wilburn (Scripture Union), and *Satan is Alive and Well on Planet Earth*, Hal Linsey (Lakeland), while *Demonology Past and Present*, Kurt E. Koch, would enable many to avoid extremes that are rapidly gaining ground in many quarters.

Yet another area in which visitors may require further advice is that of Christian counselling with regard to neurotic or even psychotic problems. It is an indisputable fact that mental illness is on the increase. The condition may be of relatively mild stress, causing occasional depression, or so severe as to cause almost constant turmoil and anguish. *The Christian Encounters Mental Illness*, Harold J. Haas (Concordia), has been valuable to many visitors who have encountered such problems. His other book, *Pastoral Counselling with People in Distress*, is also most helpful in practical advice in such counselling. Those who require further information concerning the diagnosis and treatment of various psychological problems are referred to *Encyclopedia of Psychological Problems*, Clyde M. Narramore (Zondervan). In the field of marriage counselling, *The Christian Family*, Larry Christenson (Fountain Trust) and *The Marriage Affair*, edited by J. Allan Peterson (Coverdale House), will certainly help visitors who may be called upon to counsel those whose marriages may be breaking up or have already broken up. This is a very important area to which far more Christian visitors should give attention at this present time. The home, the family, relationships between its members are some of the major issues confronting most ordinary people today. If the Christian visitor has something positive, and constructive to offer in this area he will find many open doors and listening ears!

In mentioning so many books, it is not intended to suggest that they are all essential reading for those who would visit from door to door! We are merely indicating some of the problem areas in which certain Christian visitors may feel they have been called to specialise. Would it not be helpful if certain team members were encouraged to do just this? Then as the visitors encounter various problems, they could say quite frankly: 'I'm afraid I haven't made a deep study of the subject in which you obviously have such an interest, but one of our church visitation team has done so. Would you like me to ask him to come and see you?'

It has been difficult to classify books which answer the problems concerning our faith that we may encounter in visitation work. So often the problem will relate to more than one of the fields we have been considering. Then again you may purchase a book which sets out to answer problems, only to find the particular problem you really wanted answered is not even mentioned! I am therefore going to choose three books, which between them will answer almost any problem you are likely to encounter. I am then going to list all the questions dealt with in each book. If therefore you encounter a question for which you feel you have no answer, all you need to do is refer to the lists that follow and then either purchase or borrow that book in which an answer is indicated. Some visitation teams may like to purchase all three and have them available at each report meeting. Actual problems encountered could be stated and the book answers heard and discussed.

Book No. 1. *Christian Answers about Doctrine,*
John Eddison (Scripture Union)

1   Is there sufficient evidence for believing in the existence of God?

2   If there is a God, where did He come from and where does He live?

3   Is there any purpose in men's existence?

4   Can we trust the Bible?

5   And what about the miracles?

6   Is the devil a real person?

7   Was Jesus Christ the Son of God, or just a very good man?

8   Can we believe in the resurrection?

9   And what about the virgin birth, where does that fit in?

10   What is the Holy Spirit?

11   What is the point of the Trinity?

12   What will happen to me after death?

13   Do Christians believe that Christ will come again? If so, why has He not yet done so?

14   Hasn't the church failed? And why is it so dis-united?

15   What is the difference between Roman Catholics and Protestants?

16   What is the point of the sacraments?

17   Is there literally a heaven and a hell?

18   Don't science and religion contradict each other?

19   What can Christianity offer which Humanism can't?

20   Aren't all religions equally true? Why should Christians suppose they are right, and that everyone else is wrong?

21   Do Christians believe in re-incarnation?

22   Does it matter what I believe so long as I am sincere?

23   Do we have a second chance? And what about the heathen?

24   If God is both almighty and loving, why is there so much suffering in the world?

25   If God knows everything that is going to happen, how does it make any difference what I choose?

26   How would you define a Christian?

27   Why is the Bible always harping on sin? What is it anyway?

28 If God loves us, why could He not forgive us, without Christ having to die for us?

29 Isn't it enough to follow the example of Jesus without believing that He is divine?

30 Isn't it enough if I do my best? Won't God accept me because of that?

31 How can I become a Christian?

32 How can I know whether I am a Christian or not?

33 How can I get rid of my doubts?

34 Why are so many non-Christians much nicer people?

35 Why have so many of the greatest people not been Christian?

36 Doesn't the idea of being thought 'religious' put many people off?

37 Do you believe in sudden conversion? Surely it takes a lifetime to become a Christian?

38 If God knows everything we need, then what is the point of prayer?

39 If God wants us to be good, why does He allow us to be tempted?

40 Isn't it all too simple?

Book No. 2. *Yes, But . . . ,*
    Roger Forster and Paul Marston (Kingsway Publications)

1 Why should I bother about religion?

2 When there are so many religions why consider Christianity in particular?

3 Couldn't this Jesus have been an eccentric or even legendary figure?

4 How reliable are the records we have about Jesus?

5 Is there any mention of Jesus outside the Bible?

6 How can we believe such fantastic accounts of miracles and so on, in this modern age of science?

7 Since we do not see miracles today, couldn't it be that people used to be more simple?

8 Miracles aside—doesn't the Bible contain unscientific explanations of natural processes?

10 Does this mean that you take the Bible literally—Adam and Eve and all?

11 Even if the Bible is not wrong on specific points, is not the whole view of the world according to science a different one?

12 Christians often seem to me to argue in circles.

13 Where did God come from, and what did He do before the universe began?

14 Is it rational to believe that a God of love could create a universe as full of pain as ours?

5 What about disease, is that a result of sin?

16 What of the animal world, where there is so much killing and suffering?

17 What would you say to one who is actually suffering?

18 Doesn't the Bible show a moral inconsistency between the God of wrath in the Old Testament and the God of love in the New?

19 Doesn't the Bible show an unhealthy preoccupation with blood and sacrifice?

20 If God loves everyone, then what happens to those who have never heard?

21 Then why bother to preach if all religions lead to God?

22 Even if everyone seems to have some opportunity to believe, what is the point of torturing unbelievers for ever?

23 Can't I be good without being a Christian?

24 But religious people always seem to be concerned with such silly little things!

25 Then don't you think that Christianity is narrow and restrictive?

26 But aren't Christians afraid of sex experience?

27 What exactly does it mean to be a Christian?

28 You Christians always quote the Bible, do I have to believe it all to become a Christian?

29 What would I do to become a Christian?

30 Why are there so many Christians who are racially prejudiced?

Book No. 3. *Hard Questions*,
              edited by Frank Colquhoun (Falcon Books)

1 How can we be sure that God exists?

2 Isn't one religion as good as another?

3 Can we still take the Bible seriously today?

4 What is the truth about man? Isn't the story of the 'fall' just a myth?

5 Has Christianity an answer to the problem of suffering?

6 If God is almighty, why doesn't He do better?

7 How could Jesus be both the child of Mary and the Son of God?

8 Is it necessary to believe in the virgin birth of Jesus?

9 Was it necessary for Jesus to die on the cross?

10 Did Jesus really rise from the dead?

11 Can we still believe that Jesus 'ascended into heaven' in the light of modern knowledge?

12 What is meant by the Holy Spirit?

13 Do we know anything certain about heaven and the future life?

14 Hell—fact or fiction?

15 Isn't it irrational to believe in miracles?

16 How are we to understand what the Bible teaches about the resurrection of the body?

17 What does the Creed mean by the 'Holy Catholic Church'?

18 Why is religion so dull?

19 Do you believe the devil is a real person or just a religious symbol?

20 Can prayer change the mind of God?

21 Does God ever lead people into temptation?

22 Why does the Church complicate the simple teaching of the Bible by bringing in the doctrine of the Trinity?

23 Can't you be a Christian without going to Church?

24 What is the point of the Old Testament?

25 What is meant by 'the means of grace', especially when this refers to the Holy Communion?

26 Isn't faith difficult for the ordinary person?

27 Why is the Church so hopelessly divided?

28 What historical value can be attached to the four Gospels?

29 What about the people who lived before Christ came—and the heathens who have never heard the gospel?

30　Where does the New Testament teach that infants ought to be baptised?

31　I have been baptised. Do I still need to be converted?

32　Does God give the Holy Spirit through confirmation?

33　How can we know God?

34　What do you mean by the love of God?

35　Why is the Church so much against divorce? Is remarriage after divorce necessarily wrong?

36　The Church of England seems a terribly mixed body. Does anyone know what it stands for?

37　Should clergymen be called priests? How are they different from the laity?

38　Will you please explain the second coming of Jesus?

39　Are sex relations before marriage always wrong?

40　Isn't it presumptuous to say that my sins are forgiven?

41　Ought we to lay down the law about how people observe Sunday? Surely that is their own concern?

42　Is it possible to be a Christian in the world of business?

43　Why doesn't the Church speak with a united voice on such issues as war, gambling, divorce?

44　What does the Bible mean by the wrath of God?

45　What about the day of judgment?

46　Why are my prayers so often unanswered?

47　Does God really want our worship?

48　How does Christianity affect my life in the community?

49　What is the Christian answer to Humanism?

50　Why is the Church so ineffective today?

It is suggested that in the report-back sessions after visiting, all problems encountered should be freely discussed, special attention being given to those that keep recurring.

Finally with regard to this whole subject of problems, there are three excellent group study books: *Let's Discuss, Discuss and Discern*, and *Discuss and Discover*, Hill Cotterill and Charles G. Martin (Scripture Union).

It is a pity that these books are not more well known and frequently used in study groups.

Let's Discuss considers in the main how we understand God; it is based upon the Ten Commandments. Subjects include: Sunday observance, science and creation, family life, parent-teenager relationships, capital punishment, Christian's responsibility to society.

Discuss and Discern considers how we understand the Person of Christ and provides topics dealing with moral issue arising out of a determination to live out the Sermon on the Mount, acts of God, scientific advance, the power of print, advertising, peace of mind, race relations, church unity and the price of discipleship.

Discuss and Discover considers the Person and continuing work of the Holy Spirit. It provides very full notes and further suggested reading on such topics as superstition, scientism, communism, secular humanism, the affluent society, attitute to culture, the divided church, several major religions and three deviations from the Christian faith. It will be noticed that these three books cover many of the problems encountered in Christian witness. Each book contains material for 24 topics.

First aid answers to problems, difficulties and excuses

It gives encouragement to some visitors to have ready texts and passages of the Bible which will answer problems, difficulties and excuses. This is by no means a complete answer, but a carefully chosen passage from the Word of God can often be more helpful than the most reasoned argument. Suggestions for some of these textual answers will be found in my book: *The ABC of Personal Evangelism*.

Another well prepared little booklet in this connection is *For Your Need*, a Scripture Gift Mission publication which contains several scriptures answering each excuse, false hope, doubt, false teaching, of which there are 27, quite apart from the foundation facts for the help of Christians that are listed.

The Victory Tract Club, 189 Brighton Road, Croydon, Surrey, supply a whole series of *Answer* booklets by

Leith Samuel: *The Answer to . . . Death, Defeat, Depression, Doubt, Guilt, Insecurity, Loneliness, Magic, Suffering, Uncertainty, Worry.* It will be seen by the reader that there is an abundance of literature dealing with every problem and difficulty he is likely to encounter in his door-to-door visitation for Christ.

This whole area could well be tackled by members of your visitation team. There may be problems peculiar to your district. Team members could obtain some of the books and booklets suggested and have ready the answers to share with the rest of the team as problems are related. There is no need for any visitor to feel ill-equipped as he goes from door to door in the service of Christ.

Group Study No. 12: Showing a Person His Need of Christ

Have you prayed first?

When we begin to speak to the average person about spiritual matters the main problem we often face is that he does not see himself as God sees him. He is not spiritually awakened and therefore not conscious of any spiritual need. He may know, and even admit, that he has sinned, but this may not perturb him unduly. Once a man is spiritually alerted however, he is able to respond to the good news of the gospel. He will recognise the relevance of it, in the same way as a drowning person will grasp a life belt that is thrown to him.

It is comparatively easy to gain a God-given contact in the course of our door-to-door visitation, then through occasional visits establish a genuine friendship (this can also happen of course in our day-to-day witness for Christ); but to see that friend become convicted of his need is the vital factor alone which will lead to his conversion. It is not our task to create such conviction; only the Holy Spirit of God can do so. He uses the following:

The life of the Christian worker

The outward manner of life will have a far greater impact than we realise. We ought to pray constantly that our general bearing and behaviour will be such as commend the gospel. The Holy Spirit is wanting to bear witness to divine truth being expressed through human personalities. The more we know Christ for ourselves, the more we shall express Christ in our attitudes and actions. Love, joy, peace, longsuffering, gentleness, goodness, faith, meekness, temperance—Christ can be seen in the way we live.

Discuss some situations in which such Christ-likeness may be evident. What are the problems associated with such a manner of life?

In balance with the life being lived, there should also be the word being spoken. We must watch for opportunities to tell what great things (and small things) the Lord is doing for us. We must, as we have occasion, confess to others what Christ means to us. This is basically what men are wanting today. They are wanting a spoken explanation of a new concept of life which is being lived before them! Personal witness as to what Christ is doing in terms of our daily living is one of the most neglected fields of organised Christianity. This is the 'bridge' that usually must precede the communication of the truth of the gospel.

Discuss basic differences in character between a Christian and a non-Christian. How do we explain that some non-Christians seem to be better than some Christians?

The prayer of the Christian worker

If the outward life and the spoken word constitute the manward aspect of preparation for God to work, then the inner life and prayer concern constitute the Godward aspect of preparation for God to work. If we ever hope to be used in helping others to discover Christ, and we are not only interested in 'decisions', then we must give attention to this very basic issue. To engage in any kind of evangelism, personal or otherwise, without effective prayer for the sinner is simply a waste of time. We ought to pray for specific persons by name, those we normally meet with day by day, or those who have welcomed us into their homes when we call. We obviously cannot pray for everyone, but there should be one or two 'special contacts' for whom we labour in prayer, and encourage others at the church to do at the weekly prayer meetings.

Discuss the practical questions—how can we tell those to whom the Lord is leading us to pray and communicate the gospel and how long one should continue in regular prayer for a person who appears to show little interest after all? How should we resolve such a situation?

The Christian worker communicating the truth
The spoken word may at first be little more than a testimony concerning your personal experience of Christ. To trust in such testimonies alone to effect conversions is unwise. The Holy Spirit normally uses several 'spiritual truths'; it is important however that we do not try to convey too many, rather use only one or two at a given time. We suggest that Christian workers should memorise some if not all of the following 'truths', which should be carefully 'thought through' as to how they could be applied to a friend who is showing interest in spiritual matters.

a) The *law* that we are all constantly breaking.
Matthew 22:37,38

b) The *love* that we often unthinkingly spurn. John 3:16

c) The *life* that we may be completely missing.
John 10:10

d) The certainty of *death*.   Hebrews 9:27

e) The uncertainty of *life*.   Proverbs 27:1

f) The natural life of *self centred* choices   Isaiah 53:6

g) The fact of divine *judgment*.   Romans 14:12

What other scriptures of this 'warning' nature can you recall?

It cannot be emphasised too strongly that the personal life and the prayer life of the Christian will make for the most ready acceptance of spiritual truth. A good rule to bear in mind, when visiting a person who is showing interest, is not to speak to the man about the Lord until you have spoken to the Lord about the man. This simple scriptural attitude will lift door-to-door visitation right out of the sphere of personal problems into the realm of divine possibilities!

Discuss what *illustrations* could be used to make clear the seven 'divine truths' we have listed, and share them at your group meeting.

Group Bible Study No. 13: Reminding a Friend of God's Love

Have you prayed first?

In this and the next three group studies, we shall continue to consider divine truths that the Spirit of God may impress upon a person, thus convicting him of his need. Some, for example, will seem quite unmoved when they are told of the law they have broken, but the truth of God may move them when they are reminded of the love of God which they are rejecting.

One way of communicating this particular truth is to ask your friend if he has ever seen the word G-O-S-P-E-L in John 3:16. You could then point out to him:

God so loved the world that He gave His
Only begotten
Son, that whosoever believeth in Him should not
Perish, but have
Everlasting
Life.

(John 3:16)

Or, drawing his attention to this verse, you could point out it teaches:

The greatest gift . . . . our Lord Jesus Christ.
The greatest love . . . . .the love of God.
The greatest invitation . . . .that whosoever believes.
The greatest assurance . . .shall not perish but enjoy
eternity with God Himself!

Another verse you can share with a person to remind him of the love of God is Romans 5:8. Can you suggest others?

You could consider a prophecy regarding the death of Christ

Ask your friend to read Isaiah 53:4-6 in your Bible. Ask him who the prophet was speaking about. He may be interested to know that Isaiah lived in the eighth century before Christ.

'Surely He hath borne our griefs, and carried our sorrows; yet we did esteem Him stricken, smitten of God and afflicted. But He was wounded for our transgressions, He was bruised for our iniquities; the chastisement of our peace was upon Him; and with

His stripes we are healed. All we like sheep have gone astray; we have turned every one to his own way; and the Lord hath laid upon Him the iniquity of us all'. (Isaiah 53:4-6.)

When you share a passage like this with a friend, it sometimes helps to suggest that he should change 'our' into 'my' to make the application more personal. It would then read: 'He was wounded for *My* transgressions'. What other prophecies can you recall that refer to the love of God or the sacrifice of Christ?

Consider some important aspects of Christ's death for us
The one we are praying for may be willing to have a simple Bible study with us. This is an excellent method of communicating truth which could be used by the Holy Spirit to show him his need of Christ. To consider just two or three verses could be sufficient for a single session.

(a) It was a *voluntary* death   John 10:18
(b) It was an *intentional* death   John 10:11
(c) It was a *purposeful* death   John 12:23,24,32,33

You could discuss each of these in turn with your friend. The central event of the entire Bible is the *death* of our Lord Jesus Christ. All Scripture is related to the cross; without it there could be no crown, no salvation for sinners. Beyond all doubt there was a cross, on which the young Prince of glory died. If Christ died for all—does this mean that all are saved? If not, why not? Are you then saved? What Scriptures are you resting on for peace of heart through believing?

Group Bible Study No. 14: Reminding a Friend of Man's Sin

Have you prayed first?

There has been a tendency for many years now to call sin by other names. He has a 'weakness in his character'; he is only 'sowing his wild oats'; 'Yes, he does tend to be a dominant personality'; or 'It's only a white lie after all'. Call it what we will, *sin* is a fact, and the results of sin can be read every day in our newspapers.

The plain fact is—*all have sinned*.

This truth can be communicated by asking the person you are visiting if he has consistently kept the first and greatest commandment. He may wonder what this is, which will give you the opportunity of sharing with him Matthew 22:37,38. You could suggest that he reads it himself, then ask him, 'Have you in all honesty *really* kept this commandment—all your life?' You are in fact applying the law of God to his conscience. Most men will agree that they have not kept this law and so will also agree with Romans 3:23. Intellectual assent, however, must not be confused with spiritual enlightenment.

The plain truth that all have sinned can also be illustrated by asking your friend to consider in detail the story we read in John 8:1-11, clearly teaching that none present that day would claim to be sinless. Some simple questions could be posed: (a) 'What invitation did Jesus give them?' (b) 'How many stayed to cast stones at the woman?' (c) 'Why do you think they all went away?' Having thus shared the passage with your friend, you could finally ask him: 'Could you have thrown that first stone?'

The consequences of our being sinners
Because we are sinners by nature, by birth (Psalm 51:5), we each have the tendency to commit sin in practice. A child, for example, does not have to be taught how to do the wrong thing. He is inclined to it naturally. We too find it natural to leave God out of our lives, to disobey Him, to reject His Son and to doubt His word.

(a) We are *dead* as far as God is concerned if we are not true Christians. Spiritually we are out of touch. See Eph. 2:1 and then, as an illustration of that verse, Luke 15:11-32. Notice particularly verse 32.

(b) We are *blind* as far as our understanding is concerned. We just do not appreciate the significance of spiritual truth (see 1 Corinthians 1:18). This, of course, is the work of the devil himself (see 2 Corinthians 4:3,4).

(c) We are *condemned already*. It is not as if we have to commit some atrocious sin in order to become sinners; we *are* sinners and condemned already (see John 3:18). Our natural heart of unbelief is ground enough for our condemnation.

Can you discover some other consequences of our being sinners?

The results of our being sinners

Some people with whom we speak about these things will ask, 'But why worry unduly? True, we are all sinners according to the Bible's standards, but so what?'

In Christian love you may need to share with such people one or two of the following thoughts and verses: The non-Christian—

—has no real *peace* with God   Isaiah 57:20,21
—has no true *purpose* in life   2 Timothy 2:26
—has no assured *place* in heaven   Revelation 21:26

The purpose of these brief notes is to give you a basic understanding of an unbeliever's spiritual condition. You will only be able to use most effectively such portions of divine truth as have appeared most important to you yourself. Thus you must meditate upon these great truths until they become part of you. We can testify only to that which we have seen and heard ourselves.

What other important results of sin do you think you should offer for consideration at your group meeting?

What divine truth did the Holy Spirit make most clear to you as a preparation for seeing the relevance of Christ?

CHAPTER 6

Types of Visitation

In a manual on visitation of this kind, it will be expected that not only the methods of visitation should be explained but also the different types of visitation.

If a Christian finds it difficult to conduct a Christian survey then, rather than giving up all visitation, he should be encouraged to try a different method. In a similar way, if he finds it difficult to make that first contact with a complete stranger, then perhaps he could be introduced to contacts that others have gained in order to deliver the parish magazine each month or read the Bible to 'shut in's' who have requested this.

Visitation must be conducted according to the direction of the Holy Spirit in a given area having regard to the workers available. This will not mean, however, that every worker will do what he thinks best. There should evolve within each local Church a flexible and sensitive team. The team should become alert as to the best methods of visitation to use in different parts of the town and the best type of visitation for each of its members. There is no ideal method or type of visitation ministry. The object of a manual of this kind is to outline what has or could be done and so inspire the formation of such local teams.

Very often we do not have to visit complete strangers at all in conducting a visitation ministry. Many churches have dozens of contacts by way of parents of Sunday School children, prospective married couples, contacts through women's meetings, men's meetings, young people's fellowships, confirmation candidates or those being prepared for baptism—and of course all their families. It has often been pointed out to me that the problem is not so much that of finding contacts, but finding the workers who are prepared to visit the contacts we already have! To find the workers is difficult enough, but to find the kind of workers who can communicate the gospel in a loving, sincere, scriptural and expectant way is very difficult in some churches! There are, however, various courses produced by the Fishers Fellowship designed to help Christians communicate the gospel more effectively.

The gaining of contacts is obviously insufficient of itself. It is fairly easy to gain 'friendly contacts' and to be welcome to call again whenever we like to do so. All too often, however, this can lead to a merely social visit without any evangelistic communication. True, we should not be 'pressing the claims of Christ' every time we call and there is a place for a social visit; at the same time, we must keep our priorities in order. If that person we visit does not know Christ, he has no hope and is without God in the world. If we never actually communicate the saving news of Christ and ask him what he will do with Jesus, we fail in our commission. This is the situation in which too many ministers and indeed missionaries find themselves; they visit regularly, but do not often actually communicate the gospel on a person to person basis. When they do, they suddenly find results and a spiritual explosion takes place!

We should not imagine that the presentation of the message must be some kind of programmed approach. The eternal gospel cannot be compressed into neat package form ready to be delivered at every open ear. Such methods savour too much of spiritual quackery. We are liable to swing to extremes and need to have balance in our ministry. When reminded that they seldom really communicate the message, some tend to go to the other extreme, fasten upon some contracted form of the gospel and use it at every opportunity. We should understand that there are several ways of communicating the Christian message and in most cases there are doubts, hesitations and barriers to belief that should at least be given a hearing.

The key to this whole situation in the local church is usually the minister himself. He must earn the right to be a teacher of others in the particular form of outreach in which he would like to see others involved. Here, perhaps more than anywhere, it is not a sermon his people require, but an example. If he has a loving, personal concern for the lost; if he is actually making Christ known himself; if he is personally involved in the follow-up of new converts he is winning to Christ, then and only then, can he expect others to be doing these things.

We have already thought of some fringe contacts that one may have in connection with the local church. There are also some very legitimate reasons for visitation in connection with social work, for example, gifts days of various organisations, as Dr Barnardo's Homes, Oxfam, John Groom's Crippleage, Cancer research, Tear Fund. Such visitation can always be conducted along with copies of John's Gospel or SGM leaflets. Sometimes a special 'gift day' collection of this kind can be a very helpful introduction to visitation for those not used to this ministry.

Hospital or prison visitation

With these we would include elderly people's homes, children's homes and various other institutions that might exist within the proximity of your church. In many of these places entrance can be gained and a visit will even be welcomed, not for the purpose of conducting services necessarily, but just to go and talk with the people, it may be children, who are there. There is no reason why Christians who, for example, want to visit the sick should not go along to their local hospital at visiting time and ask a ward sister to point out one or two patients who rarely receive a visitor. If a would-be hospital visitor is humble enough to accept the opinion of another Christian in confidence it would be sensible to ask for a candid view as regards suitability for this type of visitation work. More could take it up than do take it up, but it is not a ministry for everybody. Jesus said, 'Go ye into all the world and preach the gospel to every creature' (Mark 16:15). With regard to visiting the sick, He also said, 'Inasmuch as ye have done it unto one of the least of these My brethren, ye have done it unto Me' (Matthew 25:40).

Some do's in hospital visitation

Always give way to the doctors and nursing staff.

Remember hospital etiquette, e.g. not sit on beds.

Consult nursing staff before giving a patient a drink.

In dealing with the deaf and dumb, use a writing pad.

Don't neglect the unconscious person, they can some-times hear what you say.

Some don'ts in hospital visitation

Don't be noisy or frivolous.

Don't force a conversation if the patient does not wish to talk.

Don't weary a patient who is in pain, but leave a brief word of comfort, as Psalm 50:15 or Deuteronomy 33:27.

There is much literature suitable for hospital visitation. Often we find ourselves speaking to the elderly, whose sight is failing; most of the Bible Societies have large print booklets and leaflets.

The little booklets and daily reading of Peter G. Floyd are very helpful: for those who are suffering, *Beside Still Waters*; bereaved, *In Loving Sympathy*; or getting on in years, *The Beauty of Autumn Leaves*. His booklets, *Five Minutes Before You Start*, provide excellent daily readings suitable to read to 'shut-in's' or sick people before you leave them: Rev. Peter G. Floyd, The Sheiling, 7 Winchelsea Lane, Hastings, Sussex.

The 'Answer' books by Leith Samuel are also very useful to know about, to have handy and to pass on to those who raise these very common problems:

The Answer to . . . Death, Defeat, Depression, Doubt, Fear, Guilt, Insecurity, Loneliness, Magic, Suffering, Uncertainty, Worry: Victory Tract Club, 189 Brighton Road, Croydon, Surrey.

The point of this type of visitation is that not all people live in houses; some, for one reason or another, live in communities. The local visitation team therefore should be alert as to the opportunities it may have of reaching the people in such places. Just one important point: there seems always to be a tendency to think in terms of children or the elderly. We need also to concern ourselves with the middle-aged and family man. This may lead us to think in terms of 'visiting' a local social club when they have an 'at home evening', not to conduct a service, for which permission would probably be refused anyway, but simply to talk with members about whether Christianity has an answer for today. Very interesting God-given contacts could be gained in this way simply by Christians going where the people are. This kind of visitation fulfils, of course, the whole concept of outreach with the gospel.

Pre-crusade visitation

I have been involved with evangelistic crusades for many years but it is a rare thing to see such a crusade prepared for by thoughtful, well-timed and effective visitation. Nearly every crusade committee makes the fundamental mistake of starting the visitation too late, which is probably due to the fact that in most instances the publicity is not ready until a month or so before the crusade is due to begin. Also the publicity material is not designed to aid a visitation programme, but rather to advertise the crusade and to invite people to the meetings. The visitation is usually undertaken without any positive intention to evangelise, with the result that there is merely a flooding of an area with literature and a personal invitation to the meetings. The overall effectiveness of a local crusade would be greatly increased if only there were adequate, prayerful, well-timed and purposeful visitation.

Consideration of the materials being used
The visitation committee need to see produced:

(a) *A pre-visit letter*. This should be a short, friendly letter explaining that there will be a crusade, what it is all about, and that as part of the preparations a visitor will be calling back in a few days' time to conduct a Christian survey of the area. We want to know what people think about the Christian faith and its relevance today and to share our faith if given the opportunity.

(b) *A crusade invitation*. The average man does not respond to the usual mass-distributed hand-out, given him by a complete stranger, thrust through his letter-box, which invites him to a crusade meeting. Though costing more, the invitation type of card, which is given to an established contact and friend, is more likely to result in their attending the crusade meeting.

(c) *Suitable Christian communication*. We might as well face the fact that the majority of people we visit will not come to the crusade meetings. We should at least, therefore, utilise the opportunity of going to them as a time when we communicate the message *ourselves* in some way, which would be by one of the many helpful booklets that are now available: *The Reason Why* (Fishers Fellowship), *Opening the Door* (VTC), *Journey into Life* (Falcon), or *John's Gospel* (PTL). This kind of material is obviously expensive and the crusade budget may not allow for its mass distribution, but at least some should be available and visitors should know the importance of its use where possible.

(d) *Suitable Christian survey card*. Probably the best one at the moment is the one produced by YNC beginning with the words: 'Are you impressed with the works of creation?'

This material should then be collated into larger-sized envelopes, each containing 30 pre-visit letters and survey cards and 10 invitations and Christian communication booklets. The Fishers Fellowship have such envelopes ready printed with visitation instructions on the outside. Each pack will therefore contain material with which a Christian could visit 30 homes. In a united churches crusade it is not unrealistic to think in terms of 100 visitors.

Consideration of the programme of visitation

(a) The first venture-out should take place at least 12 months before the crusde is due to begin. You could arrange what could be called a Venture Day 1—a special day when as many Christians as possible from the local churches are encouraged to meet. They would hear a helpful word of instruction as to the visitation programme and all would be encouraged to take with them one visitation pack of material. They are then expected to visit their thirty homes (which could be previously noted on the packs), first by delivering the pre-visit letter and then conducting a Christian survey. They should try to undertake this visitation during the next two or three weeks.

(b) Four weeks after the Venture Day, there should be arranged a number of report-back centres, possibly in

116

different parts of the town and over two or three days at the end of the visitation period. Christian workers could then choose which centre they attend. At these report-back meetings they should be encouraged to share the way the Lord has been leading them and prayer should be made for the God-given contacts that are being discovered. The results of the Christian survey should also be collated.

(c) The crusade visitation committee would be responsible for the co-ordination of these 'Venture Days' and report-back sessions, which could be repeated several times during the year before the crusade begins. It will be realised that each time a possible 3,000 homes are being reached, and at least a third of these with definite gospel presentations. Obviously the key to the great coverage lies in the mobilisation of as many Christians as possible and the number of 'Venture Days' conducted before the crusade.

Arising from this kind of pre-crusade visitation there will be many God-given contacts; they should be reported briefly at the meetings, prayed for, and regular calls should be started. In this way most visitors will begin to establish genuine friendships, earn the right to be heard and even be able to communicate the gospel personally. Then, as the time for the crusade approaches, an invitation, using the crusade invitation card, will be more likely to meet with a positive response. Another important by-product of such pre-crusade visitation ministry is that a valuable form of outreach is being established which could well be continued after the crusade is over. Materials mentioned in this section:

Pre-visit letters/crusade invitations. These are best designed and duplicated or printed locally. Samples, however, may be obtained from the Fishers Fellowship.

Christian communications. There are several helpful gospel booklets and 'bridge of life' illustrations that could be used. Where a regular contact has been established, *The Way to God* course (VTC) is recommended.

Christian surveys. These also could be designed and produced locally. They should be kept *short* and simple. Samples of those used in various parts of the country may be obtained from the Fishers Fellowship.

Visitation pack envelopes. Plain 6in. × 9in. envelopes could be used. Instructions could be duplicated and pasted on them. Samples available from the Fishers Fellowship

Social and comfort visitation

There is a whole area of social and comfort visitation with which every local church could be involved. Social services catering for the needs of children, young persons, the elderly, the physically handicapped, the mentally ill are normally well supplied in most cities and towns. In many instances started by Christians, they are now continued through local government offices. In some areas, however, it will be found that certain aspects of social services are lacking, or the workers are without a personal faith in Christ.

Most local councils will have a Department of Social Services. These services will include: adoption service, advice from social workers, court officers, day nurseries, foster homes and foster parents, home help service, service to unmarried mothers, supportive and preventive work, children's homes, hostels, residential nurseries, bus travel concessions, club information, day centres, home meals on wheels, laundry service, night sitters, recreational advice, residential homes, accommodation, aids and adaptation of homes, clubs for the blind, disabled drivers' badges, holiday arrangements, outings, provision of telephones, talking books, wireless for the blind, after-care service, sitting-in services for the mentally handicapped. These are just some of the services that are being operated in most cities and towns today; unfortunately there are Christians who have never even heard of a lot of them.

Most of the social services are in dire need of voluntary helpers. Here is a wide-open field for social work to be done by evangelical Christians. There are several ways of going about this valuable kind of visitation.

(a)   Get to know the services that are available in your area. Take the trouble to use the telephone, write letters, make calls in order to discover exactly what provisions are being made in your area for those in need. Find out who is leading such groups and make the information readily available to your church visitors. In some places this information is already available, in others it will have to be ferreted out by one or two of your visitation team. This is such a wide field that although some lists may be available they will rarely be found complete or up to date. However, once obtained, the information can be of great value to a visitation team.

(b) The very knowledge of such services will be useful in many contacts you make. 'The world' has just the same kind of communication problems as Christians have. Many people in need just do not know that there are services in existence to help them. The informative word linking a person in need to a service that can help will be much appreciated. Apart from the help received by such persons, they are likely to recommend your visitation ministry to others. In turn this will lead to more opportunities of helping others. It will be found that this social slant in your visitation ministry leads to ever-widening circles of contact and communication.

(c) The knowledge of such services can also lead to contact with and even working for some of them. It is sometimes lamented that Christians do not enter the realm of local politics more. It is also true that they do not enter social services to any great extent. There are tremendous fields of evangelistic activity open as Christians to get involved in local social service work, not necessarily on a full-time basis, but giving for example one evening a week to it. Not only will the work give them opportunities to evangelise in the homes of the people they are helping, but also there will undoubtedly be frequent opportunities for sharing Christ with the other social workers and part-time helpers!

(d) The knowledge of such services will sometimes bring to light certain aspects that are not being catered for in your area. It may be in the will of the Lord that some members of your visitation team should prayerfully give themselves to meeting such a need, perhaps in co-operation with the local council. Councils often recognise the need long before we do, but they lack the personnel to man the project. Sometimes the local council help in a financial way by making grants to trustworthy groups, especially church-based groups who are expressing concern and are willing to help in certain areas.

Most of these social service opportunities evolve through the actual ministry of one person or a small group of people. Somebody has a burden to be of help in a certain situation; he does what he can as often as he can. He does not sit down and visualise the whole programme as it eventually takes place, nor does he move in with a ready-made answer. Rather, what he has to offer is less important than what he is himself.

Several years ago a friend of mine tentatively enquired if he could conduct a Sunday afternoon Bible Class for the young men in a local detention centre. Permission was granted. He expected that he would have only those who had a certain interest in the things of God. Instead, it happened that nearly all the boys of the detention centre were present. Christian choruses were taught and talks given by various speakers. The opportunity for Bible study courses was at first taken by a few, then more, and now most of the lads are working through these papers weekly. My friend makes a point of personally handing each paper to each lad and collecting his previous week's work. He also makes the time to answer every question raised and to check every answer given personally. By this means he gets to know each lad in a very personal and close way. Week after week he sees the lad, exchanges papers and has a brief word with him.

Some of the lads are there for a short time, others longer. One of the immediate needs upon leaving is to get a job, yet few firms or businesses will employ them. My friend, however, has gone himself to many directors of companies and staff managers and has explained the work he is doing; he has won their confidence and virtually challenged them to give 'his lads' a chance. In some cases, he tells the person concerned quite frankly, 'This one may let you down'. Over the years, however, he has built up a jobs opportunity list of which even the full-time social workers and detention centre authorities are envious. His work in one detention centre led to recommendation to others and to a prison and he is now obliged to do this work full time. It is taking him three or four days each week to answer the study papers alone.

Many, many of these lads have found Christ as their Saviour through this man's work. It is a work that not many could do and for which the highest training in theology, psychology and social science does not necessarily fit a man. Fine men, good men, trained men, could be given similar opportunities to those my friend has, but fail to do the work that he is doing.

We are obviously not all 'called' to visit the local detention centre, even if we have one! But some may be, while others may be 'called' to supply certain social services that are lacking in the area at the present time. Yet others may be called to help out with existing ones or to become involved to a certain extent with a secular set-up and communicate Christ right there among those who are seeking to help others, but do not know Jesus Christ personally.

The Street Warden Service
The Department of Social Services at Bristol are asking for clubs, groups, even churches to organise small districts so that street warden services can be established in every area. Everybody, everywhere, anytime can be a street warden! (Yes, even Christians.)

A street warden—the good neighbour stimulating other neighbours to good works! Encouraging each other to care for each other.

Not nosey—but concerned. *Not* to interfere, but ready to help in a sincerely interested way.

The street warden would visit persons in his area who were elderly, handicapped or in some way dependent on friendship from outside the normal family circle. The street warden would occasionally help with fire-lighting, shopping, making a welcome cuppa, etc.

The street warden would maintain a link with the organiser for that district so that when people wanted 'extra' help—social work advice, mobile meals, etc.—the relevant agency would be advised.

Do you want to serve your neighbour? So runs the challenge and it would seem to many Christians an obvious opportunity for visitation and making contact with people who need to know and trust the Saviour.

Helping the lonely

Social workers are constantly finding that loneliness is one of the major problems confronting many people today.

A person may work in an office full of people and spend many hours of leisure in a crowded pub yet still be lonely and in dire need of true friendship. Who can tell—except the faithful visitor—how many elderly and lonely people there are in each street, who watch the hours slowly ticking by and long for the genuine friendship of one who cares?

The following may be helpful in ministering to such people:

Never Lonely

You'll never be lonely while Jesus is near,
His comforting presence casts out every fear;
And all through life's journey, whate'er betide,
You'll never be lonely with Him by your side.

You'll never be lonely when you realise,
That the King of all glory, who built earth and skies,
Is your constant companion, so loving, so true,
You'll never be lonely while He walks with you.

You'll never be lonely though sorrows oppress;
You'll never be lonely in pain or distress;
If Jesus is with you, your Saviour and Friend,
You'll never be lonely right on to the end.

You'll never be lonely because Jesus cares,
In mansions of glory a home He prepares;
And there, re-united with loved ones above,
You'll never be lonely, redeemed by His love.

F. E. Lewis, 1955

How to avoid loneliness

1 Try to plan your day so that you don't have time when you are doing nothing!

2 Be actively engaged in doing something that helps other people directly or indirectly.

3 Develop a prayer list which you can use to pray for different people, or special ministries at certain times of each day.

4   Why not start a writing ministry and send a letter or two each week, e.g. to a young person in borstal or prison, to a person you know who is lonely or a missionary on the field.

5   Why not make a point of inviting another lonely person to a meal or round for a cup of tea occasionally?

6   Develop interests in such things as pot plants, walking, listening to a radio or TV serial, collecting stamps for missionary societies, embroidery, etc.

> I live alone, dear Lord,
> Stay by my side.
> In all my daily needs
> Be Thou my guide.
>
> Grant me good health,
> For that indeed I pray,
> To carry on my work
> From day to day.
>
> Keep pure my mind,
> My thoughts, my every deed.
> Let me be kind, unselfish,
> In my neighbour's need.
>
> If sickness,
> Or an accident befall,
> Then humbly, Lord, I pray
> Hear Thou my call.
>
> And when I'm feeling low,
> Or in despair,
> Lift up my heart
> And help in my prayer.
>
> I live alone, dear Lord,
> Yet have no fear,
> Because I feel Thy presence
> Ever near.
>
> Amen.

What to do when you are lonely

1   Practise the presence of God, that is allow yourself to become aware of His presence with you—think of Him rather than yourself!

2 Begin to count your blessings, health, strength, mobility, sight, hearing, home and memories. Thank God for each of them or for as many of them as you have.

3 Pray for others, especially for those you know who are also lonely. If you are on the telephone why not have a chat with them?

4 Claim a promise from the Bible and begin to turn that over in your mind inside of your feeling of loneliness.

5 Take up and begin to read a good book, preferably a spiritual one that will hold your interest and cause you to rejoice in God.

Bible promises for those who feel lonely at times

'Lo, I am with you alway, even to the end of the world'.
Matthew 28:20.

'He hath said: I will never leave thee nor forsake thee'.
Hebrews 13:5.

'He that cometh to me I will in no wise cast out'.
John 14:18.

'Fear thou not, I am with thee . . . I will strengthen thee, I will help thee, I will uphold thee'. Isaiah 41:10.

'As I was with Moses so I will be with thee. I will not fail thee, nor forsake thee'. Joshua 1:5,6.

'God is our refuge and strength, a very present help in the time of trouble'. Psalm 46:1.

'I will pray the Father and He shall give you another Comforter, that He may abide with you forever'.
John 14:16.

'My presence shall go with thee and I will give thee rest'. Exodus 33:14.

The foregoing suggestions, verses and Bible promises were taken from an edition of the church magazine of St. Jude, Mildmay Park, London. The editor, Rev. Nigel Stowe, wisely selected several such themes of practical interest to certain sections of the people in his parish. In these days of easy duplication the alert visitation team could produce a series of undated folders, each dealing with a particular need among those being visited. They should resist the temptation, however, of working ahead and answering the questions which are not being asked —or meeting the problems which rarely in fact (at least in their area) exist!

There is an open field in this type of social and comfort visitation, a field which most churches have never even considered. Newcomers to a district, for example, would remember who it was who took the trouble to call on behalf of the church, welcome them to the district and leave a useful folder containing information on shopping centres, local doctors, dentists, bus routes, schools, clubs, facilities and local churches. This would be appreciated (and incidentally last longer) than a single gaily coloured leaflet saying 'You are invited to our church—the friendly church. Welcome to the district!'

Immigrant visitation

Many districts today are finding a mission field on their doorstep by way of overseas nationalities settling down in this country. In going from door to door in some districts we can meet with Indians, Pakistanis, Nigerians, Jamaicans, Greeks, Jews, in fact men and women and their families from all over the world. Religions, too, will be varied; Islam (Muslims, that is believers in Islam, number about one in seven of the world population); Roman Catholicism (followers number about one in six); Judaism (the religion of the Jews, built upon part of our Bible—the Torah or Law).

Orthodox Jews will not work, travel, use the telephone, touch money or pose for pictures on the Sabbath. They try to keep strictly to the Law. Conservative Jews have a more lenient interpretation of the Torah and do not believe that the Law is vitally important. Conservative Jews also want to keep alive the Hebrew language and traditions of Judaism. Reformed Jews have departed quite some distance from Orthodoxy. They teach that the principles of Judaism are more important than the practices. Reform Jews do not observe the dietary laws or ceremonial laws concerning the Sabbath.

Hinduism is more a philosophy than a religion and there are many branches. Among world religions Hinduism occupies third place. In India 83% of the people are Hindus.

Buddhism, unlike the Hindu religion, can point back to an individual founder. Twentieth century Buddhism takes a wide variety of forms; in Tibet it is demon worship; in Japan it is the new militant, nationalistic cult of Soka Gokkai; but the two main forms of Buddhism are Hinayana and Mayanana.

If we add to these main world religions the many others and then begin to include the cults and deviations from Christianity we shall soon find ourselves with an impossible number either to know or to understand. Many religions and cults are little known by most Christians. If we find we are engaging in immigrant visitation, we shall be wise to read a few books in order to acquaint ourselves with the other 'faiths' we shall encounter.

Probably the most useful booklet at the present time is *Asians in Britain* by Patric Sookhdeo, Paternoster Press.

All visitors in immigrant areas should at least have read this book in order to gain a better understanding of the people to whom they go.

Other useful books are *So What's the Difference?* by Fritz Ridenour, Gospel Light, 27 Camden Road, London; *How to Share Your Faith with a Muslim*, by C. Marsh, Moody Press, 9 London Road, Bromley, Kent.

Roman Catholicism

Roman Catholicism Today, H. M. Carson, IVP; *Roman Dogma and Scripture Truth,* A. Stewart, IVP; *Leading Roman Catholics to Christ*, W. Ewin, Christian Publications; *Roman Catholicism*, Loraine Boettner, Banner of Truth.

World Religions

Introduction to Judaism, Lee A. Belford, Association Press; *The World's Great Religions*, Life Magazine, 1957; *The World's Religions,* J. N. D. Anderson, IVP; *Islam*, A. Guillaume, Pelican; *The Christian Approach to the Hindu*, J. C. Winslow, Edinburgh House Press; *Christian and the Great Religions*, N. Smart, SPCK; *Religions in a Changing World,* Howard F. Vos, Moody Press; *The Christian Approach to the Buddhist*, G. Appleton, Edinburgh House Press; *The Way of Zen*, A. W. Watts, Pelican; *Zen and the Christian*, J. Stafford Wright, SPCK.

Books on the cults and Christian deviations

Christian Deviations, H. Davies, SCM; *Cults and Isms*, J. Oswald Sanders, Marshall Morgan; *The Kingdom of the Cults*, Walter R. Martin, Zondervan; *Four Major Cults*, A. A. Hoekema, Paternoster; *Confronting the Cults*, Gordon R. Lewis, Presbyterian Publishing Co.

There is a real danger in becoming too involved with other religions and cults. Time is far too precious for the average Christian to spend acquiring so much knowledge of other 'faiths' which he may never profitably use in his visitation work for Christ.

Mention, however, should be made of an excellent BMMF course entitled *Who is my Neighbour*? Visitation teams working in areas where Asian immigrants will be met, would do well to take advantage of the information presented in this work programme. Islam, Hinduism and Sikhism are each given full sessions—all three, or those applicable to your area, may be used. Film strips and excellent work sheets are provided to help visitors know and understand the background and beliefs of those to whom they go.

Further details are available from: Bible and Medical Missionary Fellowship, 352 Kennington Road, London, SE11 4LF.

Revision of hints and tips in visitation

(a) To gain a friend, you must be friendly. Therefore a smile can go a long way to 'breaking the ice' and starting off on a right footing. To call at a strange home and announce what you want, or worse still, to glare as they instinctively react negatively, does not help much. It is better to go with a genuine request for help than to imply, 'I have come to help you'.

(b) Do make a point of listening. It is only by sympathetic listening that we can discover where the 'problem areas' lie. True, many are quite unjustified, but this does not absolve us from giving our time to hear them. Sometimes our very patience in hearing out a problem halves it, and the person visited begins to appreciate our call.

(c) Learn the art of asking the right questions, open-ended questions are best. Questions that cannot be answered by a 'yes' or 'no'. Asking questions, for one thing, ensures that you are not doing all the talking! It makes the person think and sometimes helps him to crystallise his vague ideas and objections and so enables you to guide him more appropriately.

(d) Never let yourself be drawn into an argument. If you do, you are being disobedient to the Scripture. 'Remember this, my dear brother! Everyone must be quick to listen, slow to speak, and slow to become angry!' James 1:19. Some non-Christians take a delight in drawing Christians into argument; but very little constructive good is achieved if this is allowed to happen.

(e) Never be afraid to admit that you just don't know. A Christian is not a walking encyclopaedia, neither is his knowledge as great as that of the Almighty. There are many things which God allows, for which we have no adequate explanation, not only the so-called 'wrongs', but also the 'rights', e.g. why life should have its enjoyments.

(f) The attitude of the visitor is very important. We must not give a hint of coldness, prejudice, superiority or patronage, especially with immigrants. We should always be open, kindly disposed; and beware of reserve which can easily be interpreted as a superiority complex.

(g) Married couples sometimes make a good visitation unit. The man can speak to men who open the door, the woman to women or children. Visiting in pairs can be helpful in training those who are unused to visiting, but it must be remembered that when two people go to a door the person who answers the call is immediately placed at a numerical disadvantage. Most experienced visitors agree that visiting alone leads to far more interesting and profitable conversations.

(h) If you are invited in, this is good and can lead to contact with others inside. Single ladies however, or ladies working alone, should be careful about going into homes, when invited by men. When visiting in districts where there are immigrants, you may be the very first European to enter their home. Accept cheerfully and thankfully food or drink that you may be offered. Learn to like curry! Don't be afraid of being asked personal questions or of asking personal questions in return. The older you are, the more respect you will command.

(i) When speaking to those from other countries, try not to use the word 'Christian' as the Asian or Jew, for example, thinks all English people *are* Christians. Try to express it in a different way, e.g. 'I am a follower of the Lord Jesus Christ, I'd like to share Him with you. . . .' Remember too, that 'other faiths' treat their holy books with great reverence. It seems odd to them to see a Christian with a 'dog eared' or heavily underlined Bible, or to see it placed on the floor.

(j) It will not always be possible to 'preach Christ' at the first visit. Each call therefore should be in some way a preparation for another. 'I have enjoyed the privilege of meeting you—may I call again?' 'Sorry, but I don't know the answer to that one, would you like me to find it out for you?' 'I can recommend a useful book/booklet and will see you get a copy.' We are arranging for those who would like to see the results of the survey to have a copy —would you be interested?' 'Thank you for your hospitality, would you like to come and have coffee with me next Tuesday morning?' 'Here, I will leave you a copy of our parish magazine and see that you get it each month.' 'I hope to come to the hospital again next week, is there anything you would like me to bring you from your home?'

Group Bible Study No. 15: Reminding a Friend of God's Judgment

Have you prayed first?

In our group Bible studies 12 to 16 we are attempting to help visitation workers in sharing the *need* for conversion. Conviction of sin and revelation of spiritual inadequacy is of course something that can be conveyed only by the Holy Spirit. The visitation worker however is a 'spiritual farmer' who goes and, as he goes, he sows the Seed. The Seed is the Word of God (Luke 8:11). Our present series of studies is designed to help in this aspect of visitation ministry.

There is the fact that everyone is going to be judged
Hebrews 9:27. 'It is appointed unto men once to die but after this the judgment.'

Nothing is so certain as death; nothing so long as eternity and nothing so foolish as not getting prepared to meet God while we have this present opportunity.

Romans 14:12. 'So then every one of us shall give an account of himself to God.'

It may be helpful to share such a verse as this with your friends. You could do it by asking a few simple questions: 'Who will be called to give account?' 'Of whom shall we be required to give account?' 'Will any be excluded?' 'Are you ready to give such an account—to God?'

What other verses can you recall which suggest, if not actually teach, that death is not the end? True, many may *think* it is, but what verses indicate otherwise? Did our Lord say anything about this matter?

How could you best apply these verses? Be prepared to share such thoughts at your group meeting.

The seriousness of neglect—it leads to inevitable loss
If a man disregards physical laws he must be expected to suffer the consequences. Who but an idiot, for example, would jump from a ten storey window and expect to land safely? The same principle should be expected to apply with regard to spiritual laws. Can a man really expect to live all his life for self, forget his Maker and escape the consequences?

Galatians 6:7. 'Be not deceived; God is not mocked for whatsoever a man soweth, that shall he also reap.'

The Greek idiom suggests that a good rendering of this verse would be: 'Don't fool yourself, you can't turn your nose up at God and get away with it!'

In Romans chapter 1, we have the solemn warning of the danger of neglect—ultimate rejection. Notice how this list of sins progresses from being unthankful to God to actually taking pleasure in those who indulge in sexual sin. Three times in verses 20 to 32 'God gives them up'—you could lightly mark these in your Bible—but it all started with a denial of God and ingratitude (see verses 20 and 21). Simple Bible studies of this nature with a non-Christian can be used to help him understand his danger. What other searching passages can you recall, or what particular truth seemed to come alive in your experience when you became a Christian?

It is important to understand that we do not manipulate such passages in order to induce some kind of guilt complex. This kind of ministry will be dependent upon the spiritual perception and sensitivity of the worker. Such truths are not intended to be driven into the unwilling mind, but to be shared with the open heart.

The warnings of our Lord Jesus Christ Himself
Ask the Holy Spirit to give you special wisdom and tenderness as you talk to people about the reality of hell. Remind yourself and your friends that the kindest and most compassionate Man who ever lived spoke more about hell than any other person in the Bible.

Matthew 7:23. 'I never knew you: depart from me.'

Matthew 23:33. 'You generation of vipers how can you escape the damnation of hell?' See also Luke 16:23.

'But surely,' we are asked sometimes, 'a God of love wouldn't cast a person into hell, would He?' The answer is that if He were a God of love only perhaps He wouldn't but He is also a God of justice. And we have to deal with God as He really is, a God whose love and justice are perfectly balanced and in righteous harmony. He does not cease to be loving when He acts in judgment.

Dr Torrey had a sermon entitled: 'God's blockades on the road to hell'. In it he pointed out the many blockades that God places in a man's way to hell: 'The Bible and its clear teaching', 'A mother's prayers', 'A kind word', 'Invitations to hear the gospel', 'Sunday School and Bible Classes', 'Christian friends and relations', 'Countless church spires pointing to heaven', 'The Cross of Christ', 'The Christian festivals'. He points out that if a man goes to hell, it will not be because God has sent him, but because he has paid too little attention to the many blockades that God has placed in his way.

Some visitors may even feel free to suggest that they themselves could be regarded as yet another blockade on the way to hell. No man can possibly say, 'But God wouldn't send me to hell!' He should consider a warning passage like this:-

'The Lord Jesus shall be revealed from heaven with His mighty angels, in flaming fire taking vengeance on them that know not God, and that obey not the Gospel of our Lord Jesus Christ; who shall be punished with everlasting destruction and exclusion from the presence of the Lord.'

2 Thessalonians 1:7-9.

In what other ways can the truth concerning the judgment of God be conveyed to a person we are visiting? When is the best time to share such a solemn subject?

Group Bible Study No. 16: Reminding a Friend of the Emptiness of Life

Have you prayed first?

One of the oldest questions that has engaged the mind of man is: 'What are we here for?' Closely related to this question is man's inherent desire for something (some One) outside himself. 'Man is incurably religious', said one, and this is true. This is evidenced in the fact that a man is either found worshipping the God who made him—or the god that he has made. His own god may take many different forms.

Augustine, an early church leader, said:

'Thou O Lord, hast created us for Thyself—and our heart is restless until it finds its rest in Thee.'

Discuss this observation in your group study. In what ways is it evidenced today? How do men endeavour to find 'heart rest'?

What other verses or passages can you recall to illustrate this truth of man's incompleteness without a personal faith in God based upon the finished work of Jesus Christ?

Pictures of incompleteness and frustration

The Bible, you can explain to your friend, contains some remarkable pictures of those who had everything, but still did not find real satisfaction and fullness of life.

Solomon, for example, had the opportunity to experiment with:

Pleasure—wine—wisdom—architectural works—nursery farming—orchard planting—pond making.
He had servants—possessions—treasures—musicians—'whatever my eyes desired I kept not from them.'

Ecclesiastes 2: 1-10.

But then notice his conclusion in verse 11.

The Prodigal Son had a similar experience: Luke 15: 11-19.

Just a simple consideration of this story with a friend can impress a truth far more deeply than we realise at the time. What other passages of this nature can you recall, which could be used to illustrate what we mean by the unsatisfying nature of the Godless life?

It is not always realised that the non-Christian life is basically unsatisfying. Many have so constantly stimulated their jaded senses that they actually imagine that they are rich and increased with goods, and have need of nothing; and they know not that they are wretched, and miserable, and poor and blind and naked in the sight of God.   Revelation 3:17

We have some very interesting pictures of the Godless life.

> 'You have sown but you bring in little,
> you eat but have not enough,
> you drink but are never filled,
> you dress but you are not warm,
> you earn wages to put into a bag with holes!'
>
> Haggai 1:6

Can you think of some contemporary illustrations?

In Jesus Christ alone we can enjoy fullness of life

> 'If any man be in Christ, he is a new creature—a new creation—old things are passed away, everything has become fresh and new!' 2 Corinthians 5:17

We can explain that the natural man, a non-Christian, is really a divided personality. He is incomplete, not all there. His interests are controlled by 'self' which is variable and results in discord and confusion. Self interests are constantly changing and divisive. The pleasing of self often causes the displeasure of others.

In Christ however, that is when a person is united by faith to Christ, the lesser personality yields to the Greater. The result is unity; the true Christian alone is complete, whole! His interests are controlled and subsequent to those of Christ. This results in direction and purpose in life. Paul could say, 'this one thing I do. . . .' When a person becomes a Christian he begins to fulfil the purpose for which he is here. It is rather like a disjointed bone suddenly being put in its right position. This is what our Lord meant when He said:

'I am come that they might have life—and have it more abundantly'.   John 10:10

Not much life can be released through a bone that is out of joint! Make a list of three ways in which the abundant life of Christ can be seen in the life of a true Christian.

Your personal testimony concerning what a difference Christ is making in your life (provided it can be seen by the way you live) is one of the most convincing evidences of the relevance of the Christian message today. Our manner of life should be such that men are convinced when they meet us, of the emptiness of life apart from personal faith in Christ.

CHAPTER 7

In-Depth Communication

Many Christian churches have for many years been concerned about the lack of new converts that are being added to them. It is not unusual to find some churches or assemblies, where months, even years, go by without even one new convert being added to them. The reason for this is not difficult to find. The fact is that the Lord does not add 'new converts' to the 'church' as we know it. The actual church building or place of worship is normally added to only as new families, already Christians move into the district and begin to worship there. Their gain is someone else's loss! Rarely do we find that a complete outsider, a non-Christian, begins to worship at our church and eventually becomes a member of the fellowship.

In the days of the apostles, we read, the Lord added to the church such as should be saved; the church however to which they were added was not a building of bricks and mortar, but rather the local body of believers. It has always been the plan of God to add new converts to the converted, as a result of their obedience in making known the faith.

The basic reason why the Lord is not adding to many churches today appears to be simply because the local companies of Christians are not being obedient to their heavenly calling and are not discharging their divine responsibility. God is saying 'go' and we are saying to the people 'come'. It will often be found that the paucity of evangelistic results in any church or assembly is directly related to its scarcity of united evangelistic outreach. The Lord said to the early Christian, 'Go . . .', and we read, 'They went everywhere preaching/communicating the Word'.

Nowadays churches may commonly be likened to a fortress more than a team of fishermen thrusting out in their boat to catch fish! There is about the typical church a certain brittleness, an established order of tradition, a strange regimentation, and even an archaic language. At the appropriate hour each week, it is as though we let down the drawbridge and almost dare the outsider to come into our citadel and join us. If they do, then they find some of the happenings a little odd, to say the least! Some are aptly calling this type of evangelism 'in grab evangelism' as it is in fact reaching only those who do come in. The Scripture has stated for many years now, 'He which soweth sparingly shall reap also sparingly . . .' What shall we say then of the local church that is hardly sowing at all, as far as those outside are concerned?

God is sovereign and He will have His Word proclaimed, if not by those within the churches, then by His people outside the churches. This explains why it is, that in almost every generation, there are those who come together from various churches (usually, but not always, the younger age groups) who have a practical concern for those who are without Christ. They recognise that the 'church' is not effectively reaching the people outside at all. Such groups find themselves without the restraints of formalism and ritualism and simply get on with the job of evangelism. The Lord begins to add to their number, and there appears a crop of new converts. There are those being added to Christ in that outreach fellowship, but not necessarily in the local church. This is what happens when we have the occasional evangelism explosion, so often outside of, and apart from, the church as we know it. Many of the denominations, sections of the church, and special ministries now being conducted by societies, began in this way.

It is as simple as this, if God is not allowed to evangelise through the local church, (which we believe is the scriptural pattern), then He will simply raise up a man or a group of believers who will evangelise outside and apart from the local church.

Every local church fellowship therefore should reconsider this whole subject of outreach evangelism; In what ways for example is your local church fulfilling our Lord's command, 'Go ye into all the world and proclaim the gospel to all mankind?' How can your fellowship best be motivated into action? What are the best methods of outreach, having regard to the district and workers available? Have you formulated a clearly defined strategy for moulding your membership into a 'communicating fellowship'. It seems strange that most churches have a man or a committee, specially appointed to care for the finance, the publicity, the magazine, the notice board, the women's meeting, the Sunday school, the youth fellowship, the flower rota, the cleaning and even the catering—but so few have a committee for evangelism! Yet this is one of the primary purposes of the church being set in that particular district. 'Evangelise or fossilise' is an oft repeated slogan and it's right. If your church is not evangelising, it is fossilising.

The basic principles of evangelism are simple and easy to understand. It is we who so often make them more difficult than they really are by our plain disobedience. By not going where the people are we have the problem of getting them where we want them! By not telling the truth of God as it really is we sometimes have to resort to psychological manoeuvres or salesmen's techniques in order to elicit a response. There should be no need for so many conferences, seminars, congresses, workshops and teach-ins on evangelism. Evangelism is the work of the whole church for the whole age; it consists simply of local Christians going where the people are, telling them of God's standards and man's failure, sharing Christ, His life, death and resurrection for our sins, and inviting men to repent and believe. This of course should be done each day as we have opportunity, without causing social offence. But it should also be done in some way by the local Christians as from their own fellowship and as a united outreach action. It is by this means that so many are finding door to door visitation most effective. Where such a definite outreach action in evangelism is being accomplished faithfully and prayerfully, governed by sanctified common sense, the Lord will undoubtedly be adding to the church again such as should be saved.

A fault which is sadly common among church

members who do begin to think about evangelism, is a pre-occupation with elderly people or young children. This will obviously lead to an additional reaping from those age groups. To whichever age group or type of person we take the message, we ought not to be surprised if it is from these that we reap the larger portion of new converts. If, for example, we persist in our evangelistic endeavours among the drug addicts, the drop outs and minority groups, exciting as the work may be, we ought not to expect to find a reaping of new converts from normal, balanced persons. If our main concern in evangelism is with women and children, we ought not be surprised if we have few men in our congregations! Bearing these principles in mind, it is not difficult to understand why churches normally seldom see new converts among married couples and men. If we expect to reap from such sections of the community, then we have got to sow among those sections of the community. This is why I am writing this book. I believe there is no better place for reaching the normal person than right in the home where he lives. We have no need to get them to come or go any where. It is our privilege to speak to them about Christ right there in their own homes.

Communicating the gospel to a God given contact

Door to door visitation is merely the means whereby we are able to gain 'God-given contacts'. Now there are many ways, methods and reasons for making that initial call. We obviously have to discover the one we personally find most helpful in the district in which we are visiting. The whole point of the calling however is to place ourselves where God can lead us to a person of His choice. Every so often in our visitation work we shall find ourselves speaking to a person obviously prepared of the Lord for us. Of course there will be those who are 'not interested' or 'haven't the time', but there will also be the person for whom the Lord has a message through our lips. The gospel may indeed be communicated on the doorstep at the first visit, but it is more likely to happen when that contact has become a genuine friend of the visitor and begins to confide in him or her.

The actual ways in which we see that our friend 'hears the Word', by which he could be saved, are many. We may take the gospel to him ourselves, which, incidentally is more scriptural, or having gained his confidence we may be able to get him to go to a place where he can hear it preached. The latter is far more difficult but it is the only method that most Christians would think of using. If we take the gospel to our friends, then it can be seen in our lives, heard from our lips and possibly passed on to be read in various kinds of literature.

Some Christians prefer to learn by heart a pattern approach or chain of texts through which they can conduct their friends. Some agencies produce booklets or even teach complete dialogues containing all the possible answers to all the possible questions we could hear in making a gospel presentation. Others prefer to discover the extent of the faith, or doubt, of the person first and then work from *that* point. Yet others find illustrations like the 'bridge of life' or 'four spiritual laws' very helpful in getting across the gospel message. The fact is that the Lord can use all and any of these ways of conveying 'saving truth' to a person who is disposed to listen. We limit ourselves if we insist upon using only one way.

Showing the need of Christ to a person

Once the contact has been established and regular calls or visits are being made, making known the gospel is a matter of person to person evangelism.

There are several helpful books available on this important subject.

Fishing for Men, Major Batt (IVP)

You Can Witness with Confidence, Rosalind Rinker (Lakeland)

How to Give Away Your Faith, Paul Little (IVF)

The ABC of Personal Evangelism, Ron Smith (Send The Light)

Everyday Evangelism, Ron Smith (Send The Light).

It is possible to share our need of Christ as we speak of the great truths concerning the love of God, the sinfulness of man, the certainty of judgment and the emptiness of life without Christ. You will find a fuller exposition of these great Bible truths in the Group Bible Study outlines at the end of chapters 5 and 6 of this book.

You should as well be praying regularly for the person you are visiting. It would be helpful if you could relate your progress at your weekly church prayer meeting, so encouraging others to pray specifically for you and your friend as you meet. This kind of praying can add real interest to the local prayer meeting.

Your life also will be used of God to reveal a 'sense of need'. According to the measure in which divine truth is part of you, it can be expressed, sometimes quite unconsciously, to the person you visit. On the other hand, there ought to be times when you quite definitely communicate the truth concerning his need of Christ. You can share what God has said concerning standards, unbelief, life, death and judgment to come. Take your time, be courteous and avoid argument. Be humble and don't be ashamed to admit your ignorance on certain matters. Maintain a sense of humour; sometimes you will need it! Don't be afraid of giving your personal testimony. Tell your friend just how and why you came to trust Christ yourself. Make your spiritual experiences relevant to today's world. Use your Bible, remembering the message is not yours but the Lord's. His Word is the agent of conviction and conversion. Let the interested person begin to read for himself as soon as possible the particular truths to which you want to draw his attention. The revelation of his spiritual need is something for which you should be praying and working first. It may take one visit, it may take many visits; it will depend upon the way in which the Lord goes with you and confirms the Word, spoken by you in the heart of your friend.

On some occasions you will probably call and hardly even mention spiritual matters, simply pass on your usual monthly literature or ask if you could take a short Bible reading before you leave the home. At other times you may have a long conversation about almost everything, except the things that matter most. If however you find that you never speak about the Lord and salvation, obviously in that situation you are not involved with direct evangelism at all. You must make opportunity, either by means of asking questions or by using a questionnaire of some kind.

In the very nature of visitation evangelism, you will find there are far more contacts than you can possibly follow through by regular visitation so you will have little difficulty in choosing those with whom you are finding your visits more fruitful in gospel communication.

The content and communication of the gospel

When it comes to the content of the gospel or the basic facts to which the sinner should assent, there are many such plans and programmes. The emphasis should be shifted from one point to another, depending upon the need of the individual concerned. Sometimes only one or two points will need to be covered. At other times the whole plan may be known in the head, but never have been made known in a meaningful way by the Holy Spirit in the heart.

Communication of the gospel involves a telling or a teaching situation. Again this *can* take place during one interview, but it is usually better to take place over a period of time. Most people today are altogether ignorant of the basic facts of the Christian message and the true facts concerning Christ. It is therefore normally helpful if these truth are explained in detail during a series of meetings, rather than in one 'on the spot' presentation under pressure.

Here is a suggested plan which has been used of God. It could be covered and discussed over a series of six visits.

1 *The fact of sin* Romans 3:23
We need to convey the fact that we have all sinned in God's sight. What is sin? 1 John 3:4, James 4:17, John 16:9. Why worry? Romans 7:19, 2 Corinthians 4:4, Isaiah 59:2.

2 *The fact of judgment* Hebrews 9:27
We need to convey the fact that *God* is *just*. He must execute judgment upon all sin. There is a *Hell* to be avoided as well as a *Heaven* to be gained.

3 *The fact of salvation* John 3:16
We need to convey the fact that *God* is *love*. He has made

provision for the guilty sinner through the substitutionary death of our Lord Jesus Christ.

4   *The need for true repentance*   Acts 3:19

Point out that *repentance* is essential to salvation. This means turning from self and sin, forsaking unbelief and everything that is offensive to God.

5   *The need for sincere faith*   Acts 16:31

Point out that *faith* is also essential to salvation. God has spoken—and offers—*Christ*. It is by faith we accept Him for what He claimed to be—co-equal with God, and we confidently trust *Him* alone for our acceptance with God.

6   *The need for personal response*   John 1:12

Point out the need for a personal encounter with the Lord Jesus Christ. Many believe, but have never received Him. It may be helpful at this point to provide an opportunity for a response to be made. This must never be forced in any way. Our responsibility extends only to the faithful delivery of the message and invitation to respond to Christ.

See Acts 2: 36-40, 8: 35-37, 10: 38-43 and 26: 23-29.

To obtain a clearer conception of what actually constitutes the gospel read *The ABC of Personal Evangelism* in which you will find some more comprehensive Group Bible Study outlines covering various aspects of gospel truth, e.g. redemption, regeneration, justification, faith, the sinfulness of sin and the death of Jesus Christ.

There can be no stereotyped approach. Every approach, however, must eventually terminate in *Christ*. Here are some more useful steps to bear in mind.

Notice how the four steps of this particular presentation can easily be recalled by the alphabetical order of the verbs—Admit, Believe, Consider and Do.

1   *Something to admit*

That we are sinners and unable to get ourselves right with God.

Sin —a falling short. Romans 3:23.

Guilty —sin separates us from God and brings us under His just judgment.   Isaiah 59: 1-2, Romans 6:23.

Helpless —we cannot be saved by our own efforts at right living or good works. Isaiah 64:6, Ephesians 2: 8-9.

2 *Something to believe*

That God, in the person of Jesus, lived as a man and died to save us. His ability to be our Saviour is based upon the following:—

(a) His position and person as the 'Go-between'. 1 Timothy 2:5.

(b) His death in our place for our sins. Isaiah 53: 5,6 and 1 Peter 2:24.

3 *Something to consider*

That acceptance of Jesus Christ as Saviour involves surrender to Him as Lord of the life.

True commitment to Christ involves:—

(a) Repentance—a turning from sin.   Acts 3:19.

(b) Dethronement of self.   Mark 8:34.

(c) Surrender to Christ.   John 13:13; John 20:28.

4 *Something to do*

An act of the will, by which we encounter Christ personally. This can be:—

(a) A 'coming' to Christ.   Matthew 11:38; John 6:37.

(b) A 'receiving' of Christ.   John 1:12; Revelation 3:20.

(c) A 'believing' on Christ.   John 3:16; Mark 9:24.

It is suggested that you consider carefully these two plans, the one in six steps and the one in four steps. Adapt one or the other, possibly with changes of references to use it as your own. Make an outline of it with references on a piece of card and keep it in your Bible. Use it in your day to day witnessing for the Lord and door to door visitation.

Your plan need not become a rigid system in communicating the gospel, but the very knowledge of such a plan will help you in making the message clear and plain. It is simply because they have no such clear concept of the gospel themselves, that many Christians and some ministers find it difficult to communicate.

There are various 'natural' starters to a spiritual discussion, for example, 'the state of the world today', or 'why there is such a lack of genuine love and concern for each other'.

Here are some other facts with which you could start a useful conversation.

(a) Over half the world will go to bed hungry tonight—who is to blame?

(b) 7,000 people starve to death every day, while a disproportionate few are living in luxury—why is this?

(c) In the United States, every block in Hollywood has a psychiatrist.

(d) Two out of three hospital beds have a mental patient. One out of three marriages ends in divorce. Crime is continually on the increase and England is not far behind. Is this civilisation?

You could then explain that the essence of true Christianity is concern for these things and the central theme of the Bible is love. Here are some thought-provoking verses:— Mark 12: 29-31; John 3:16; 1 John 3: 14-19; 1 John 4: 7-21, many verses from the Sermon on the Mount (Matthew 5-7) and any of the Ten Commandments (Exodus 20).

Show how each commandment can only be kept as we love God and one another. Another helpful pair of verses is Matthew 22:37,38. Ask your friend, before showing him this verse, what *he* thinks is the greatest commandment of God. Then the very consideration of these two verses can be used of the Holy Spirit to show him his need. You will not have to tell him, for the Holy Spirit may have done so—he is a sinner in the sight of God, and he will know it. It is by your Christian life, your prayers and the communication of God's Word and standard in this way, that your friend may begin to recognise a missing factor in his or her life. You will sense that he is prepared at least to listen to the good news concerning Jesus Christ.

Yet another difficulty some Christians encounter in communicating the Christian message is the inability to make points clear. Some find it hard to convey spiritual truth in a way that their friends can understand.

One way of overcoming this particular problem is to become acquainted with the truth as it is presented by those gifted to do so. Note their illustrations and how they build up their reasons for the faith. Two excellent books to use for this purpose are:

Who Died Why?, John Eddison (Scripture Union).

Right with God?, John Blanchard (Banner of Truth).

We are now going to take five basic themes, which could constitute yet another plan of salvation. Alongside each of these themes we are placing the parts of the above books that deal with each theme. Once again, you could make a note of the five themes on a postcard, then read the appropriate passages in each of the books. You will discover that certain illustrations or points really do become helpful and clear to you. Make a note of them on the postcard. This is the first step to your being able to make them clear to others.

1 'Christian or not a Christian?'
   Who Died Why?   Chapter 3,   pages 24-31.
   Right with God?   Chapter 3,   pages 30-46.
2 'What is this thing called sin?'
   Who Died Why?   Chapter 2/3,   pages 7-23.
   Right with God?   Chapter 2,   pages 14-29.
3 'Does sin really matter?'
   Who Died Why?   Chapter 8,   pages 68-76.
   Right with God?   Chapter 2,   pages 14-29.
4 'What has God done about sin?'
   Who Died Why?   Chapter 4,   pages 47-89.
   Right with God?   Chapter 4/5,   pages 32-49.
5 'What does God expect me to do?'
   Who Died Why?   Chapter 6/7,   pages 50-67.
   Right with God?   Chapter 5,   pages 90-113.

Having regard to the three foregoing plans containing the essence of the gospel, no Christian reading this book can fairly say, 'Having discovered a God-given contact through door to door visitation, I don't know the gospel clearly enough myself to communicate it to another person.' Too long have we left gospel proclamation to the preachers and neglected to communicate the message from person to person.

Other methods of communicating the gospel we could use

Pictorial illustrations
In our present TV age, many people receive knowledge better through what they see than what they read or hear. This may account for the growing popularity of

hand-sized visual aids. *Four Steps to Life, Your Destiny* (YNC), *Four Spiritual Laws* (CCC), *Journey into Life* (Falcon), *The Bridge of Life* (FF), *The Little Green Book* (VTC). Door to door visitors should know about these, how to explain them, and then begin to use them occasionally in suitable situations.

Pre-conversion courses
Many contacts we make as we go from door to door are willing to investigate the faith for themselves by means of a course of some kind. Several years ago we were able to pilot such a series of courses for the unconverted. Further information on these pre-conversion courses may be obtained from the Fishers Fellowship.

Christian literature
This is another area that is greatly neglected as far as gospel communication is concerned. There are some excellent gospel books and booklets that should be made known to visitors and be available for loan or sale as required. Every visitation team should be kept up to date as to what books are available and could be used in connection with door to door visitation. Sometimes when entry to the home is not extended, a monthly call with *Challenge* or the parish magazine is welcomed. Then after some months a booklet or book could be given to the person being visited.

Messages on tape
Mention has already been made of the potential of this form of communication. There is no reason why the visitation team themselves should not produce the kind of programmes that would be appreciated and have them available on cassettes. Obviously in a home with children and other members of the family watching a TV programme, we cannot suddenly ask for the set to be switched off while we play a cassette recording, but in some visiting situations it would not only be possible but appreciated!

Person to person study course
There is a very useful course obtainable from the Fishers Fellowship. It is intended to be an aid to visitors in homes. It is called *The Way to God* and covers the five

themes already referred to in this chapter. It is designed to help the visitor to communicate effectively, at least part of the gospel each time a call is made. The whole gospel is thus clearly presented over a period of time. Only the basic thoughts and relevant Scriptures are given, the idea being for each worker to adapt the course to suit the need of the person he is visiting.

Presenting a person and the place of response

It will have been seen that there are many ways of presenting the gospel. These should be clearly explained to all visitation team members, so that they can begin to use the methods which they find most easy and find most helpful in certain situations. We now come to place of response. Following the communication there should always be a challenge to do something about the truth heard. Upon the announcement of the good news, there should always be an appeal to believe it. With the statement of the gospel, there should always be the summons to embrace it. Becoming a Christian really involves the receiving of two truths and then responding to a Person—Jesus Christ. Truth one is concerning our *need* of salvation, and truth two is concerning God's *provision* of salvation. It is important that we should encourage devotion to a Person rather than assent to a creed.

The Word of God is the *seed* that saves.

Luke 8:11 and 1 Peter 1:23.

The Son of God is the *One* who saves.

1 John 4:14 and 5:1

Having communicated the gospel it is not enoug
imply that a person becomes a Christian if he bel
what has been presented. Hundreds have done t
it simply leads to mental 'believism'—there ha
surrender of the will and enthronement of
wrong 'Jesus', a mere mental image, is
and confessed. The right 'Jesus', the
Jesus, the Jesus of the Bible, is God-
ance, denial of self, and a disciplined
ship.

How to counsel a person to faith

(a) Discover the extent of

want to become a Christian? Why? Does he realise that he has broken God's law? Does he know that he will have to give account to a holy God? Mere interest is *not* enough. If he is not sure of his *need* of Christ, then you could share with him Matthew 22:37,38, Romans 14:12 or Hebrews 9:27.

(b) Discover the extent of his understanding concerning our Lord Jesus Christ. What does he believe concerning Jesus, whose Son is He? Why did He suffer on the Cross of Calvary? Was any fault found in Jesus? What happened three days after His crucifixion? Who was Christ and where is He now? Mere intellectual knowledge is not enough. There should be evidence of divine revelation coming through. Matthew 16: 15-17.

You may need to share with him verses that speak of the virgin birth of Christ, His sinless life, His divine sonship, His voluntary offering of Himself, His substitutionary death, His glorious resurrection, His ascension to the Father or His soon coming return!

You will have noticed that two important revelations by the Holy Spirit are required:

    (i) That he knows that he is a needy sinner, and

    (ii) That he knows that Jesus Christ is an all sufficient Saviour.

The place of accepting Jesus as Saviour and Lord
You may need to explain that saving faith involves both ̶b̶e̶l̶i̶e̶v̶i̶n̶g̶ ̶a̶n̶d̶ receiving. It is possible to believe in Christ

̶ ̶ ̶ ̶Him.

̶h̶is place of deci-

̶h̶e either accepts

̶g̶ it off. 2 Corin-

̶g̶ a decision.

̶n̶ audible prayer.

̶n̶d spoken confes-

̶m̶ans 10: 9,10.

̶e̶ who respond by

̶n̶se is made, your

̶n̶ning. Continue to

̶n̶d communicate in

other ways to those who have as yet not responded. You will obviously reach the place with some where you have communicated the gospel several times and no response has been made, then, like Paul, you must turn to others who have not heard the Word so clearly. Your ministry to such people may bear fruit at a later date.

This whole matter of in-depth communication is the key to an effective and soul-winning visitation ministry. Visitation team leaders should make sure that every team member is given instruction in the ways of making the message clear and plain, and frequent check ups made to see that the visitors are really communicating.

Further help in the areas of personal evangelism and follow up may be obtained from my books:

The ABC of Personal Evangelism

(Send the Light Trust)

The ABC of Follow Up　　　　　　(Send the Light Trust)

Group Bible Study No. 17. The Gospel That We Have To Communicate

Have you prayed first?

The word 'gospel' means 'good news'; it comes from the two Anglo-Saxon words, 'god' (good) and 'spell' (news). We are all acquainted with the 'gospel in a nutshell': 'For God so loved the world, that He gave His only begotten Son, that whosoever believeth in Him should not perish, but have everlasting life' (John 3:16). In this verse we see the basic elements of God's good news. God loved the world and gave Christ. Man's part is to hear and believe.

Discuss the question: 'How can I help the person who says he has heard and does believe in Christ yet is obviously not a true Christian?'

The heart of the gospel (and it is well to remember this in a day of many other 'gospels') is the substitutionary, atoning death of our Lord Jesus Christ at Calvary. That so great a sacrifice was required should emphasise our sense of need. Jesus Christ was without sin, yet He was treated as a sinner. He kept the law of God perfectly, yet upon Him was laid the iniquity of us all (Isaiah 53:6). He was made sin for us (2 Corinthians 5:21 and Hebrews 9:28).

We shall now consider some basic elements of the gospel in the form of questions and answers. You should answer each question from the Scripture given—but in your own words.

Why does man find it natural or normal to displease the Lord? Psalm 51:5.

How many have sinned in the sight of God? Romans 3:23.

When may we expect judgment to take place? Hebrews 9:27.

What is the nature of divine judgment upon believers? 2 Thessalonians 1: 8,9.

How does God make provision for our forgiveness? Isaiah 53:6.

What is the great proof of the love of God toward us? John 3:16.

What does God expect of us as our first step toward Him? Luke 13:3.

What must we then do to become 'children of God'? John 1:12.

What does 'following Christ' involve concerning ourselves? Luke 9:23.

What is the evidence of a person 'believing in the heart'? Romans 10: 9,10.

Having answered these questions yourself, be prepared to share some of your answers with other members at your next group meeting.

Is there any other aspect of gospel truth you feel should be conveyed also as we communicate the message? Would you say it is necessary to believe or obey it also for salvation? Notice carefully the response required by our Lord (Mark 1:15), by Peter (Acts 2:38 and 3:19) and by Paul (Acts 17:30 and 20:21). Do we expect this kind of response today?

How can I help a new convert to grow in the faith?

Leading a person to faith in Christ is one thing, but seeing that person become a responsible member of the local church is another. The problem, however, if there is one, is that of our own making. The more traditional or unrelated to everyday life our church services are, the more difficult it will be found for some people to conform to them and to find them helpful. The new convert, however, will be found perfectly at ease and able to grow naturally within the context of ordinary Christian home fellowship, Bible study and witness groups.

I do not think personally that the answer is for us to stop traditional church forms and services, or even to change them unduly, but rather to concentrate on person to person discipleship strategy to the stage where communal worship is recognised for the real value it has. It is really a matter of time and patient continuance in well doing on the part of the visitor. It means visiting that new convert at regular intervals, conducting a series of person to person discipleship studies, and seeing him established in the faith and really taking in the Word of God. It also means helping him in the matter of daily quiet times and expressing his faith in personal witness for Christ. He will then soon enough begin to realise that the lone Christian is at a disadvantage and begin to look upon his local church as his spiritual home.

Once again we need to remind ourselves of what the Word really says. It does not say that the disciples added to the church such as should be saved, but that the Lord added to the church. In the usual course the real Christian will find his way into the local fellowship of believers, just as naturally as the non-Christian finds his way into the local fellowship of unbelievers!

Ways to encourage Christian growth

1 Urge your friend to trust what the Bible says rather than how he may happen to feel. Suggest that he memorises a verse like John 5:24 as soon as possible.

2 Explain to him the importance of open confession of his faith in Christ. Show him Romans 10: 9,10, or Matthew 10:32. Discuss with him the value of letting people know Whose we are and Whom we serve.

3 Don't forget to pray for that new convert. Ephesians 1: 17,18 and 2: 17,18. Encourage others in your local fellowship to pray for him too.

4 Remind him that he is only beginning the Christian life. There are many lessons to learn. A Christian is, after all, a *disciple* which simply means a learner! Make sure you arrange future visits when you can share with him some basic discipleship lessons (2 Timothy 2:2).

5 Give him an appropriate counselling booklet. The Fishers Fellowship have seven of these, they are designed to meet the needs of various ages—children, teens, students and adults.

6 Continue to visit your new convert as often as you think reasonable. Each time you go make a point of having a definite Bible study with him. See *Going on with God* as suggested below. You should of course invite him to your local church, but don't pressurise this as both reasons and motivation will come out in your studies together.

7 Introduce him to other keen Christians of his own age or profession. There may be sectional meetings of your local church in which he would find an initial interest—a men's meeting, YPF or home Bible study group.

8 Remember the ministry of good helpful Christian literature. Send the Light Trust, 9 London Road, Bromley, Kent will gladly send a book list and make helpful suggestions. (There is also a list of helpful books for new converts in *The ABC of Follow Up*.)

9 Remember the ministry of Christian Radio programmes. There are helpful Bible Studies to be heard every day from Trans World Radio. Write to Trans World Radio, c/o The London City Mission, 175 Tower Bridge Road, London SE1.

10 If there are a number of new converts, consider the possibility of starting a discipleship class or home study group. The Fishers Fellowship provide several group study notes for this purpose.

Person to person follow up

We believe the most effective follow up is done by a person, preferably the person who led the convert to Christ in the first place, although it should be recognised that in most visitation teams the workers will have different aptitudes, which should be used to the full. It may be best in some cases for the original visitor (the spiritual midwife) to give way to a follow-up worker (a spiritual foster parent). *Going on with God* is the title of seven simple study sheets recommended for this kind of follow up provided by: The Victory Tract Club, 189 Brighton

Road, Croydon, Surrey. Full instructions for use are contained in each pack and such subjects are covered as assurance, Bible intake, communion, dependence upon God's promises, endeavouring to adjust our lives to God's Word, fellowship with local Christians, and going to tell others about Christ.

Following this series of studies there is *Bible Doctrine*, and after that there is *Winning Another*. These three courses will provide material each week for more than six months of a new convert's life in Christ.

This then is what we mean by our chapter heading— *In-Depth Communication*. Through visitation the contact is made, the gospel is proclaimed, the opportunity for response is offered, and, where it is accepted, the way of God is explained more fully until that person becomes mature in Christ and is reaching others. What of those who do not respond as we hope? We simply continue to visit as we have opportunity, continue to communicate the gospel, perhaps in different ways, but like the apostle Paul we realise that not all will obey the gospel and some will consider themselves unworthy of everlasting life. The point may be reached when we must turn our prayers and attention to others. This is our commission and our calling, we cannot save the lost—one plants, another waters, but it is God, and God alone, who gives the increase.

Group Bible Study No. 18: The Follow Up of Converts

Have you prayed first?

Read carefully the introductory passage to this study from Acts 15:36 to 16:5. Notice how Paul evidently considered follow up very important. So it is according to the practice of the early Christians (Acts 10:48,11: 23, 13: 43,15: 41,18:10,27 and 20:28-35). We believe that those whom the Lord saves He is able to keep, but this does not absolve us from our responsibility toward every new convert. God is pleased to use us to feed, help, protect, encourage and instruct those who have recently given their lives to Christ.

Evidence of Regeneration

When a person is born again of the Holy Spirit, we should expect new motives, new principles and new objectives to control and direct his life.

From the following Scriptures discover some evidences that the new birth has in fact taken place. Write them in your own words. 1 John 3:14; 1 John 5:18; John 14:21; 1 Corinthians 5:17; Galatians 5:22,23.

What other evidences of new birth can you recall?

Essentials for Christian growth

Christian growth is dependent upon our personal relationship to Jesus Christ. Our knowledge, devotion, faith, obediences and service 'in Him' should be increasing continually. This actually happens in our experience as we learn to adjust our lives daily to God's will as revealed in His Word. We expose ourselves to the Truth of God, and if our attitude is right and our heart is tender, the Spirit of God can work God's will through us. Discover from the following Scriptures some basic growth-producing factors. Write them in your own words.

John 9:25.	Hebrews 10:25.
Acts 17:11.	John 15:4.
John 14:23.	Romans 12:1,2.
John 16:24.	Mark 16:15.

What do you consider to be the three most important of the above? If you could encourage a new convert in only one of these, what would it be?

Examples of Apostolic follow up

Read carefully 2 Timothy 2:1-26. Then discover some principles of the apostle Paul's follow-up programme.

(a) He visited converts in person.
    Where did he go to do this? Acts 15:36 and 41;
    Acts 18:23.

(b) He sent another where he could not go himself.
    What did he say concerning such persons? Philippians 2:19,20.

(c) He made a point of writing to the converts.

The Second Epistle of Paul to Timothy and the First Epistle of John contain some of the finest counsel available to young converts. Which of these epistles would you suggest should be read by a new convert who needs assurance, and why?

What particular passage or which verses did you find very helpful as a young Christian? Be prepared to share these at your group meeting.

(d) The apostle Paul prayed regularly for new converts.

Select four definite petitions, one from each cluster contained in the texts given. Ephesians 1:17; 2:17; 1:18; 2:18.

Jesus said: 'Lovest thou Me? *Feed My Sheep.*'

Life Change Studies

Life Change Studies is a weekly personal Bible study course, published by Send The Light Trust. It is in two volumes, each volume providing a balanced series of Bible studies for each week for two years.

Life Change Studies do not present any 'loaded' denominational teaching. The student is expected to consider all the scriptures he can find in order to compare scripture with scripture and thereby obtain a pure biblical theology.

Life Change Studies should be available from your local Christian Bookshop.

CHAPTER 8

The Use of the Home

Our main interest in the home in this manual has been as a place to which we go in order to gain contacts for Christ. There is, however, another very important aspect of the value of the home—it is that of a 'meeting place', other than the church itself or the church hall.

The Christian's use of his home has contributed tremendously in both evangelistic and faith building endeavours. There is about the home an informality, a friendly and natural atmosphere, that is not normally experienced elsewhere. The very fact of being able to sit in easy chairs, especially in a cosy room, generates a closeness of fellowship. The home too, is often more accessible than the church; clearly this is most likely to be for those who live in the vicinity of the home in which a meeting is being held. We all know as well how a stranger is more likely to come to a near neighbour's home than he is to come to the church. Refreshments are more easily prepared, the china is usually more attractive, children are more easily cared for. It is significant that the New Testament notes that in the early church the believers met in each other's homes. Home meetings have frequently been centres of spiritual blessing.

The objective of the home meeting

We ought to be clear from the outset as to exactly what the objective should be. Too many home meetings seem to be allowed to take their own form and have no clearly defined objective at all. If no one has the goal in view, it is unlikely that the goal will be reached.

There are basically three objectives to bear in mind for a proposed home meeting; to communicate the gospel to the unsaved, to provide a nursery for new converts and to provide fellowship in growth and outreach for Christians. In some cases it may be necessary to combine some of these objectives, but in every case the convenors should know exactly what they hope to achieve by having the home meeting.

Important principles to remember

(a) If we are convening a home meeting for non-church goers, we must try at least to be contemporary with regard to the name we give it. 'Talk Back', 'Sit Inn', 'After Eight', 'Talking Point' or 'Pop Inn' would obviously have a greater appeal and be more meaningful than 'Home Meeting'.

(b) The invitations should be far more personal than they usually are. To flood an area with leaflets inviting strangers to a 'Home Meeting', or even using a more contemporary name as above, will not bring much more response than doing the same for a church meeting. Non-church-goers are not exactly waiting to be invited even to a Christian's home, unless the home happens to be in a wealthy district, owned by a star or stage or screen, public entertainer, TV personality, politician or wealthy businessman.

The home meeting should be looked upon as a gathering point for those who are being visited regularly and who already have taken an interest in the message. In some areas a 'Challenge Get Together' for those who have been receiving *Challenge* has proved very successful.

The printed invitation card is therefore to be recommended rather than the handout leaflet. Incidentally, not all people appreciate the gaily coloured kind of dazzle card, which some printers are in the habit of producing in their efforts to bring the Christian image up to date!

(c) It will be found wiser to plan for a series of home meetings and then stop, than to start something which merely drags on and eventually dies a natural death. Such a short series of home meetings will also encourage more specific prayer support from your local church. In some cases a bi-monthly evangelistic home meeting could be followed by a short series of follow up meetings in that home.

(d) Speakers can sometimes be a very disappointing conclusion to an otherwise good home meeting. A poor speaker can completely negate all the good efforts by visitors to get a friend or a neighbour to the meeting. Particularly to be avoided is the type of speaker who puts the outsider on the spot and gives the impression it is now or never!

Very often the ordinary Christian who can share quite naturally what Christ means to him day by day is more suitable than the 'well known personality' who can convey a kind of 'professionalism', to which some easily take exception.

The speaker should be chosen with regard to the kind of people expected. If they are regular church attenders, fringers or those who have previously heard the gospel, then it may well be right for the speaker to challenge them to respond. If on the other hand, they are friends and neighbours, to whom the visitors are just beginning to communicate the gospel, then care must be expected. To be suddenly thrust into a home meeting situation where the speaker is calling for a response, when those addressed hardly know the truth to which they should respond, have a spiritually abortive effect! This too is one of the dangers of many popular youth outreach efforts today. Contact is being made with those 'outside' but the content of the communication is lacking. The average church of course by means of their Sunday evening service accomplish the very opposite!

The whole matter of suitable speakers can be quite a problem. One answer is to invite the kind of speaker who will be prepared to speak not longer than fifteen minutes on a specified theme and then to open up the subject for discussion. The talk back situation is constantly being seen and heard on TV these days and is in wide use in many establishments of learning, but not it seems the Christian church. We must remedy this; speakers must learn to listen as well as to speak. Also when he does not know the answer to a question or problem a speaker should have the humility to admit it.

(e) It is very important to keep strict control of the

timing of a home meeting. No good is achieved by delaying the start until the main company has arrived. People will soon recognise that a meeting does not start until they arrive, with the result that it will begin later and later. A prompt start should therefore be made at every meeting, even if there are only a few present at the appointed time. Then also, a definite time at which the meeting will close, should be made known and observed. We should realise that not all present may be entering into the spirit of the discussion; they will then begin watching the clock, and if the proceedings do not close on time and this is their first experience of a home meeting, it might also become their last!

Types of home meetings

We are now going to consider some of the types or forms that a home meeting can take; these are not to be confused with the aim of the meeting. The aim or objective must clearly be defined first:

(i) evangelistic, (ii) discipleship, or (iii) Christian fellowship.

Once the objective has been defined, then the convenors can decide which of the type outlined below will best meet the objective they have in mind.

(a) Bible study led by a teacher

A Bible study can be an acceptable method, even in the case of non-Christians. We are wrong to imagine that all non-Christians are opposed to a Bible study. The very idea of going to a neighbour's house at the invitation of a Christian friend, whom they have come to respect, can have a great appeal to many people. Most people are not opposed to the Christian faith and probably consider themselves Christians anyway. *The Way to God* course (VTC) could make an interesting syllabus for a five week course. If those attending were also asked to consider the relevant passages from the two books, *Right with God* and *Who Died Why?*, then a more effective way of getting the message across could scarcely be conceived. This, remember, is the kind of method normally employed at confirmation classes or baptismal classes.

(b) 'Passage Plough' and verse by verse study papers

The papers are mainly discussion starters. At the same time, however, a good amount of Christian truth can be gained from the study of the passage chosen. It will be found best to give out the study papers a week before the actual meeting, as it gives each person the opportunity of working on the questions before they come together. Although the method is not ideally suited to non-church-goers, nevertheless many non-Christians appreciate this kind of 'free for all' home meeting, where they can say exactly what they feel concerning the passage under consideration. We must be careful in such situations not to allow any who hold erroneous doctrines to 'take-over' the home meeting!

The Fishers Fellowship produce several of these 'Passage Plough' and verse by verse study papers. Samples will be sent upon request. Write to: The Fishers Fellowship, 96 Plaistow Lane, Bromley, Kent, England.

(c) The Harvester Group Bible Study Notes

These notes are also produced by the Fishers Fellowship and cover a range of subjects including Christian living, basic doctrine, personal evangelism, problems to the faith, door to door visitation, follow up of new converts and the second coming of our Lord Jesus Christ. There are fifteen separate study sheets to each of these subjects. It is intended that each group member shall be given the 'Harvester Group Study' paper, which he or she can complete privately before the actual meeting. It is not necessary to work through a subject completely and leaders may choose subjects in whichever order they prefer.

Your own denominational bookrooms will probably have similar group study material, as will the following societies:

Billy Graham Evangelistic Association, 27 Camden Road, London, NW1.

Campus for Christ Crusade, 105 London Road, Reading, Berks.

Inter Varsity Fellowship, Norton Street, Nottingham.

The Navigators, 86b Coombe Road, New Malden, Surrey.

Scripture Union, 5 Wigmore Street, London, W.1.

(d) The invited speaker or demonstrator

In some areas there is a Christian actor, doctor or politician. This sometimes provides the opportunity of inviting several of the same profession to hear how he relates his faith in Christ to every day life in the professional world.

The home meeting for God given contacts need not be an occasion for directly communicating the faith at all; book evenings, cookery demonstrations, discussions of parent and child problems, musical evenings all can have their place and time in the 'home meeting' scene. Avoid the mistake, however, of *only* amusing, educating or entertaining God given contacts, remember our primary task is to present each person with the claims of our Lord Jesus Christ.

(e) Film strip or film evening

This form of meeting will lack the 'drawing power' it enjoyed several years ago, but such visuals can provide a useful means of gaining interest and promoting discussion. Most of the denominations have their own visual aid departments. If you should find difficulty in obtaining material of this nature, write to the following asking for their catalogues:-

Church Army, 185 Marylebone Road, London, NW1.

Church Pastoral Aid Society, 32 Fleet Street, London, EC4.

Concordia Publishing House, 117/123 Golden Lane, London, EC1.

Gospel Sound and Vision, 44 Georgia Road, Thornton Heath, Surrey.

The Scripture Union, 5 Wigmore Street, London, W.1.

We are in fact inundated with such material. Scripture Union alone has a vast amount of material to suit all kinds of meetings. One of our biggest problems is to keep abreast of what is available!

Gospel Sound and Vision have a useful series of film strips suitable for children. They have several interesting stories of places where these film strips have been used and the numbers attending have just kept increasing until the home or the hall could hold no more!

(f) *Musical evenings—bring your own discs!*

This could well prove to be the type of home meeting which many God given contacts would attend. Your 'descriptive title' for the evening will naturally depend upon your likely supporters! Some could bring their own discs, and you can always feed in a sufficient number of discs to get across a spiritual message. To close such an evening in a Christian home, there is no reason why you should not have an epilogue of an appropriate character. Similar evenings could be arranged for various kinds of interests discovered among God given contacts, such as hobbies, travel, sport, languages, art, common hopes, fears or ambitions.

(g) *Talk-it-over groups*

Probably the simplest kind of home meeting is the talk-it-over group. No detailed preparation is required, as this kind of meeting is normally the sequel to the Sunday services. 'The Bitter Enders' it was called in one place. The group, usually the younger element, who seem disinclined to go home but want to remain together preferably in a church member's home. Irving Harris of 'Faith at Work' has had much experience of this type of informal meeting. He has the following to offer.

(i) *Start small.* Jesus made no prior announcements. He sought a person here, another there—some fishermen, a tax collector, a number of others and brought them together to talk, to work and to pray. Why should we try to improve on this?

(ii) *Go deep.* Someone has said, 'Dogma, denominationalism and social respectability have largely overlaid the spirit of love . . . the average Church fellowship is so respectable that the real problems never come out into the open'. In a small intimate fellowship people's real problems are aired more easily. Honesty often leads to help and Bible truth, instead of being presented theoretically by an expert, is often revealed in living form by a novice.'

The talk-it-over group is of supreme help to young Christians, provided that it is not allowed to become *only* a guitar-strumming, chorus-singing session, but definite spiritual matters are discussed, prayed over and daily witness for Christ experiences openly shared.

The home meeting has a definite value for Christians and a limited value for those who are beginning to show interest or who are church fringers. It is, however, almost useless as a catchment ground for complete strangers to whom we think we can preach the gospel (or at least a speaker will) once we get them in a home together. The greatest value of the home meeting lies in its informality and the ease by which we can get to know people as persons.

Suggestions for further study in this subject:

Break Through, Tom Rees (Hildenborough Trust).
Home Bible Studies, Derek Copley (Paternoster Press).
Know How to Lead a Bible Study, J. Hills Cotterill (Scripture Union).
Reading the Bible Together, H. Wilson (Church Information Press).

The ten commandments of a good home meeting

1 Decide exactly what objective you have in mind.
2 Prepare by prayer and common sense, invitations to friends.
3 Keep strictly to the time schedule you have planned.
4 Be enthusiastic and friendly to all, especially strangers!
5 Don't talk too much but encourage many others to participate.
6 Learn the art of asking the right questions to promote discussion.
7 Be firm with the continual talker; keep control.
8 Never argue or take sides in a controversial discussion.
9 Use plenty of sound and visual aids.
10 Do not be afraid of brief silences, as quiet reflection is good.

It will become very enlightening if, after every home Bible study you lead, you ask at least two persons present (whose opinions you respect) which three of the above commandments, in their estimation, you failed to fully observe.

Time To Advance

The notes which follow are intended to provide actual study material for a series of five group meetings for committed Christians. The object of the exercise is to encourage personal outreach within the context of daily Christian living. The notes are introduced at this point in the manual because they are probably most helpful when used at a series of home meetings. They may, of course, be used (as they have in the past) to replace the usual midweek Bible study at the local church. The success of these studies will depend to a large extent upon the leader of the group. He should be a person who recognises the value of group sharing and discussion and is prepared to keep silent himself and encourage group members to share their experiences. Some groups have found it better to meet every other week.

The leader will need to provide definite instruction for ten to fifteen minutes on the main topic under consideration at each group meeting. This could be a prepared talk by a minister, pastor or other Christian leader. There is a special cassette produced by the Fishers Fellowship called *Time To Advance*. It contains five of the radio talks, suitably chosen to provide the five instruction talks for the group sessions. It could take the form of a tape recording (e.g. one of the Fishers Fellowship radio programme tapes, now available on cassettes). It could simply be a tape-recorded reading from a suitable passage in a book on personal evangelism. It is important that this instruction period be kept within twenty minutes. It has been found that the main value of *Time To Advance* lies in the sharing of the ways in which the assignments are being fulfilled. Normally a deep prayer fellowship is generated and frank discussion arises from the questions being answered. There are now plenty of tapes, books and courses available for those Christians who want to know how. Our greatest need at the present time is not more knowledge, but more personal action, more sharing of experiences and prayer for individuals. This cannot be gained from books or taught by a speaker—so do keep the instruction period short. Never let the 'instructor' exceed his limit, otherwise precious time will be used in listening, which could have been better employed in sharing personal experiences of witnessing, discussion and praying for individuals.

Each member of the group should have a copy of this manual. They should be asked to study the relevant group study personally before each meeting. Answers to questions should be written out, and the group leader should make a point of asking for some of these. No one, however, should be made to feel embarrassed if they have not answered all the questions or completed every assignment.

Time To Advance—first week

Theme: *The Christian and his personal preparation*

(a) Here are four questions we should like you to consider, and then write out your answers, ready to share with other members of the group if called upon by the leader when you meet for your first meeting.

What are the main qualifications of the personal evangelist?

Why do Christians find it so hard to witness for the Lord?

What motives ought to cause us to share our faith with others?

In what ways can we expect the Holy Spirit to lead us in witness today?

(b) The second part of your *Time To Advance* group will be taken up with some form of definite instructions as prepared or arranged by your leader. Each period should last approximately twenty minutes.

(c) In many ways this is the most important part of the evening—the prayer time. It is hoped that this prayer time will become more 'alive' as definite contacts are being made and prayed for, and up to date news of them is being related each week. The first week, however, prayer should be made (i) for the success of the *Time To Advance* venture as a whole, (ii) that your leader will be helped in his preparation and leadership, (iii) that group members will become concerned for those who are lost and diligent in their personal studies and assignments. Pray too that other members of your church will yet be given the desire to take this course and become more effective in reaching others for Christ.

(d) Telling is not teaching, neither is listening learning. Thought must result in action. Lessons must be expressed in the life. Theory ought to be worked out in practice. It is expected from now on that each member of the study group will try to fulfil the suggested assignments set for each week, and then at the next group meeting be prepared to relate his or her experiences in so doing. The next two assignments should be completed between your first *Time To Advance* meeting and the second.

Write out what the difference is that Christ is making in your life at the present time (say 100 words). It would be helpful if you came prepared to read this out at the second group meeting if called to do so.

Memorise verses 19 and 20 of Matthew 4.

Time To Advance—second week

Theme: *Making the approach—gaining contact.*

(a) Here are your four questions. Write out your answers and be ready to share them with the other members of your group at the second meeting.

What exactly do we mean by the word 'evangelism'?

Suggest several ways we could begin a spiritual conversation.

What are the characteristics of a good approach?

How does the Bible describe a person who is not a real Christian?

(b) The second part of your *Time To Advance* should be taken up with some form of instruction as prepared by your leader.

(c) Some group members should be invited to read their papers on 'The difference Christ is making in my life at the present time'. Opportunity should then be given for group members to share experiences they have had in making contact and speaking for the Lord during the past six months.

The leader should then check various group members to see how well they have memorised the first memory verses, Matthew 4: 19,20.

(d) It will be noted that the prayer period from now on will occupy the last part of each evening. Prayer will become more specific now as actual individuals are being prayed for and contacts are being made by group members. Pray that every member of your group will have several definite opportunities to speak for Christ during this coming week. This is a very important part of our advance—we must learn to speak to the Lord about the man, before we speak to the man about the Lord.

Assignments for next week (to be completed between the second and third meetings).

We all have opportunities to speak for the Lord in the course of our everyday lives. It is expected from now on, as the Advance continues, that each group member will take these opportunities as they occur. He should be willing to share these experiences at the next group meeting. 'What he said' and 'what I replied' should be simply and frankly related.

One of the best methods of gaining a contact is, as we have stressed in this manual, visitation. Try this method. Take out ten copies of *Challenge* newspaper, and deliver them to ten homes without calling. Call back in two or three days' time, introduce yourself and say which church you are from, and then ask the occupant if he would like to receive *Challenge* each month. If this is done in a prayerful, friendly way, you will find that some will agree to receiving the paper regularly. (It would help if a simple explanatory letter could be delivered with the *Challenge*, but this isn't essential). You will probably discover some opportunities in the course of this action for speaking to people about the Lord. Having visited the ten homes in this way, make a brief note of the kind of responses you obtained and be prepared to share these at your next group meeting.

Memorise Matthew 22: 37,38.

Time To Advance—third week

Theme: *Helping a person to see his need of Christ*

(a) Here are your four questions. Write your answers

and be ready to share them with other members of the group at your next meeting.

What exactly do we mean by the word 'gospel'?

What are the blessings enjoyed by becoming a Christian?

What are the four main facts concerning sin that come to your mind?

How can we help a person to see his need of Jesus Christ?

(b) The second period of your *Time To Advance* should be taken up with some form of definite instruction, relative to the general theme, prepared and arranged by your leader. Are you keeping this instruction period short? The four periods of each *Time To Advance* evening should be approximately of the same length—fifteen to twenty minutes each. Those accustomed to longer evenings together could lengthen the periods to thirty minutes, but it is important to maintain a four period balance.

(c) Group members are now invited to share their actual witness experiences (i) in relation to the normal everyday living; simple accounts of how a conversation began can be very helpful at this stage. Try to keep reports as up to date as possible, preferably for the period since your last group meeting. Problems encountered should be openly told and discussed, unless they are of a confidential or private nature. Then (ii) in relation to the visitation exercise with *Challenge* newspapers. How many were delivered in all? How many occupants agreed to receive it each month? What kind of conversations started from this door to door ministry? How many obtain what could be called God given contacts where they could call again? Don't forget to arrange for regular distribution where required.

(d) The prayer time. There may be a tendency at this stage to relate experiences in witnessing to the extent that the prayer time is trespassed upon: this must be resisted. The leader must make a point of insisting upon brief and to the point reports and must ensure that at least the last quarter of the time spent in the group meeting is spent in specific prayer, praise for the contacts being gained and petition for specific cases of real interest. Pray for those members of the group who will be meeting these contacts again, possibly during the next week. Pray that every group member will have the opportunity to communicate the Word of God to at least one person before the next group meeting. If time check last week's memory work.

Assignments for the next week

The basic law of God is contained in Matthew 22: 37,38, which you will have memorised as part of your assignment for last week. This is God's standard, and by it all stand condemned. No one has attained the moral and spiritual perfection required by this law. Continue making contacts by conversation this coming week, and try to share with at least one person this law of God. Remember to speak the truth in love and be prepared to relate some of the reactions you encounter at your next group meeting. Was he offended? If so, in what way? Was he offended at you or the law? Did he agree with the view that if all have failed to keep it, then all have sinned? Did anyone claim to have kept this first and greatest commandment? Would you say that the Spirit of God had made the truth meaningful? Why? If not, is there anything else you can do?

Time To Advance—fourth week

Theme: *Presenting the good news of the gospel*

(a) Here are your four questions:

How would you answer: 'But I do not believe there is a God'?

How would you answer: 'But I do not believe the Bible is true'?

What are the main elements of the Christian gospel?

How do you find it most easy to convey the Christian gospel?

The group leader should continue to watch carefully the fourfold division of time at each group meeting. It is important that they be kept about equal.

(b) Instruction period as arranged by the leader.

This should include, this week, explanations of various ways in which the Christian message can be made 'clear and plain', as the old hymn puts it.

(c) We should now like to hear:

(i) of new contacts that have been made since the last *Time To Advance* group meeting.

(ii) of specific instances where you have communicated the truth concerning the law of God, which reveals a man's need of Christ. Names of contacts should be noted on a blackboard (or other visual) so that the group members can pray specifically for such individuals during the prayer time.

(iii) from group members who can repeat by heart all three memory verses we have taken thus far. Notice the purpose of each.

(d) In the will of the Lord, it should now be possible to pray for those who are showing a genuine interest in spiritual matters. Pray that the interest will become God-given conviction and enlightenment. Only God can cause the seed to germinate but He has commanded that we sow it. Pray especially for those group members who now have good contacts, that they may be granted spiritual perception and clear guidance as to what they should say or do when they see these persons again. Pray too for the problem cases, the difficult types and those who seem to be unmoved or even antagonistic to the gospel. Finally, remember to pray for any discouraged workers.

Assignments for the next week

The basic truth concerning redemption is contained in 1 Corinthians 15: 3,4, which you will have memorised as part of your assignment for last week. This is God's provision for man's sin. In your contacts and conversations this week, try to share with one person, at least, this great redemption truth: 'Christ died for our sins, He was buried and raised again; He is alive!'

You should have been instructed in other ways of communicating the gospel. Why not watch out for opportunities to use one or two of them this coming week? Be prepared to relate some of your witnessing experiences at the next group meeting. It would be helpful if you could have ready brief answers to the following. During the week how many conversations about Christ did you have? To how many did you communicate last week's law? To how many the way of salvation?

You will notice that our *Time To Advance* themes are

following a definite pattern. Communion—our personal walk with the Lord. Making contact—how to begin a conversation. Conviction—revealing the need by declaring the 'law'. Communication—sharing the good news of God's provision. In our personal work, however, we must not in our thinking restrict the ministry of the Holy Spirit. John 3:8 is still as true as ever. The worker himself must be rightly related to the Lord before he can be used. Conviction of sin and need normally, but not always, precede our appreciation of the gospel.

Memorise John 1:12.

Time To Advance—fifth week

Theme: *The challenge to respond and follow up*

(a) Here are your four questions:

What are the main problems that face a new convert?

What are the six most important means of Christian growth?

What are the advantages of fellowship with other Christians?

How did the apostle Paul follow up his converts?

Your answers to these questions should be noted ready to be shared at your fifth group study.

(b) Instruction period as arranged by your leader.

This should include simple directions for leading a person to faith in our Lord Jesus Christ.

(c) We should now like to hear:

What has been happening since the last *Time To Advance* group meeting? Can each member relate (i) an example of making a new contact and speaking about spiritual things? (ii) an example of sharing with a person our need of Christ, because we have failed to keep God's law? (iii) an example of communicating the good news of the gospel? (iv) Who was able to use a 'Bridge of Life' illustration? (v) Who was able to give a gospel booklet?

(d) It may be possible in the will of God to begin giving thanks for those who have trusted Christ during the past few weeks. It must be remembered, however, that 'salvation is of the Lord'. Our task is to be faithful in sowing the seed as we have opportunity. By this time the prayer sessions should have become very meaningful.

Personal action in the cause of Christ with names and persons to mention, situations and events to recall, all gives substance to our praying. It will have been found that definite prayers result in definite answers!

Suggested assignments for the future

(a) The members of the *Time To Advance* group will have discovered the value of sharing personal experiences each time they meet. Some groups may want to continue meeting on a regular basis, of not every week, then perhaps every other week. Some may find it better to divide into several smaller groups, meeting in homes. Others may decide to stay on occassionally for a *Time To Advance* group meeting after a church service.

(b) Follow up, the 'discipling' of new concerts and young Christians, is extremely important. It forms the basis of expansion in evangelism. Every Christian should be personally helping each week at least one new convert or other Christian younger in the faith. The most practical way of doing this is to obtain a set of *Going on with God* person to person Bible studies (VTC) and to conduct the new convert or younger Christian through them.

Memorise 1 Peter 2: 2-5.

The Fishers Fellowship provide these *Time To Advance* group study notes as separate duplicated sheets. Kindly note that they should not be reproduced locally without written permission.

Fishers Fellowship Tapes

The following cassette tapes contain instruction on personal evangelism given by Ron Smith, originally produced for the radio programme *In Thy Name We Go* (Trans World Radio).

These tapes are available in Christian bookshops or direct from STL Message Tapes, Mail Order Dept., P.O. Box 48, Bromley, Kent, England.